Youth policy in Cyprus

Conclusions of the Council of Europe international review

Daniel Menschaert (CDEJ)
Anca Sirbu (Advisory Council)
Peter Lauritzen (Council of Europe)
Ditta Dolejsiova
Yael Ohana
Stanko Salamon
Howard Williamson

French version:
La politique de la jeunesse en Chypre
ISBN 978-92-871-6227-4

Council of Europe,
Directorate of Youth and Sport
European Youth Centre
F-67075 Strasbourg Cedex
Tel: +33 (0)3 88 41 23 00
Fax: +33 (0)3 88 41 27 77
e-mail: youth@youth.coe.int
http://www.coe.int/youth

Cover design and page layout: Desktop Publishing Unit, Council of Europe

Council of Europe Publishing
F-67075 Strasbourg Cedex
http://book.coe.int

ISBN 978-92-871-6048-5
© Council of Europe, August 2007
Printed at the Council of Europe

Contents

Preamble

"Cyprus, according to mythology, is the birthplace of the goddess of love and beauty, Aphrodite. The island is both an ancient land, with an 11 000-year-old history and civilisation as well as a young independent Republic since 1960. Its geographic location at the crossroads of three continents – Europe, Asia and Africa – and at the meeting point of great civilisations, has been one of the factors influencing the course of the island's history throughout the centuries." (About Cyprus, Republic of Cyprus Press and Information Office 2001, p. 18)

All international reviews of national youth policy generate distinctive challenges for the review team. Irrespective of their composition, knowledge, expertise and experience, to 'make sense' of a country's specificities – its social, political, cultural and historical traditions – through visits that are rarely more than two weeks long, and through reading a range of disparate material, is always difficult. Given the particular conditions and circumstances that prevail in Cyprus, it has been especially difficult. The international review team found itself seeking to unravel what at times appeared to be an 'impenetrable complexity' of policy and practice in relation to the young people of Cyprus – at the levels of governance, data, provision and outcomes. The team encountered many competing and often contradictory perspectives, inconsistent and often incomplete information, and the inevitable, overarching presence of the 'Cyprus Question', to which we shall return, though it is not within our mandate to comment directly on what remains an apparently intractable political dilemma.

Nevertheless, it is within that political framework of the Cyprus Question that its young people – from the Greek Cypriot and Turkish Cypriot communities, from the minor religious groups of Maronites, Armenians and Latins, from the settler communities in the north and the new 'immigrant' communities on the island – are having to live their lives. The Cyprus Youth Board, established a decade ago, has sought to develop a framework of policy and practice to meet their needs. It has done so with considerable success, attracting significant praise from disparate quarters, though many of its developments remain relatively new and are still in the process of consolidation.

At the time this report was being prepared, Turkey was seeking to strengthen its candidature for membership of the European Union, a position achieved by Cyprus in May 2004. Not surprisingly, the continuing illegal occupation of the north of Cyprus bore heavily on that discussion, though – as with Cyprus' own accession to the EU – the resolution of that 'question' is not a pre-condition for future progress towards EU membership. It will nevertheless, no doubt, hang over further developments, just as it has been a pervasive feature of our own reflections. For, as the press spokesman for European Commissioner Gunter Verheugen commented in March 2003:

> "If, by the time of the report at the end of 2004 there is still no settlement on Cyprus, we are facing this rather weird situation where a candidate country knocking at the door does not recognise one of our own member states." (Republic of Cyprus Press and Information Office 22.3.04, p. 6)

Cyprus is, however, not alone in having to address division and difference, both within and beyond contemporary Europe. The 'bi-communal' aspirations on the part of some in Cyprus have striking parallels with the 'cross-community' initiatives developed over many years in Northern Ireland. Division is premised upon a complex mix of ethnic, religious, territorial and constitutional tensions, resonant of regions of the Caucasus, former Yugoslavia, the Middle East, and indeed, New Zealand, where the Treaty of Waitangi continues, some two hundred years on, to provoke argument between the Maori and white '"settlers"' over questions of 'sovereignty' and 'governance'. Thus Cyprus is by no means unique in struggling to find an acceptable platform for resolving its thirty-year-old problem, whose antecedents go back considerably further.

Nor is the position of Cyprus at the crossroads of continents and civilisations unique. Malta (whose youth policy was reviewed by the Council of Europe in 2003) would stake a similar claim. Thus, though the various contexts affecting Cyprus are not unique, they do present a distinctive constellation of issues – among which some specific concerns were expressed in relation to young people. These included their new place within the European Union, the implications of thirty years of division and conflict, and a growing concern about illegal drug misuse. The international review was interested in both locating these issues within a wider context and interrogating their meaning and prevalence within the specific context of Cyprus, in order to reflect upon the current and potential policy response.

The international review team has sought to offer a 'stranger's eye', one that endeavours to place the Cyprus Problem at arm's length (however difficult that may be) and put the context of young people in Cyprus at centre stage. Young people in Cyprus are now, uncontestably, an integral cohort of European youth, for whom a critical and outward-looking imagination is essential if they are to serve well both their own interests and those of the communities in which they live:

> "The future of European culture depends on its capacity to equip young people to question constantly and seek new answers without prejudicing human values. This is the very foundation of citizenship and is essential if European society is to be open, multicultural and democratic." (European Commission 1995, p. 10, quoted in draft National Report on Cyprus, chapter on Culture, pp. 3-4)

In this spirit, the international review team engaged with various interpretations of the 'social condition' of Cypriot youth and endeavoured to, in sociological parlance, render the familiar strange – to generate a critical reading of current circumstances while applauding areas of innovation. In the language of non-formal educational practice, this report tries to move all players in youth policy in Cyprus into a 'stretch' zone – beyond the 'comfort' zone, but short of a 'panic' zone that tends to paralyse rather than promote reflection and development.

Youth policy in Cyprus

Youth policy, as a concept, was routinely conceded to be relatively new in Cyprus, though it needs to be stated from the outset that it is relatively new – as a coherent and integrated concept – everywhere. This report may note, in some domains of youth policy, that Cyprus is still on the starting blocks, but in other respects it is commendably ahead of the game. The international review team hopes its analysis will provide a catalyst for consideration of new development in some domains and a confirmation that, in other domains, initial development is moving in a constructive and purposeful direction.

The international team was aware of the strong commitment in Cyprus to formulating a more robust and rounded approach to 'youth policy'. The Cyprus Youth Board, in its response to the European Commission's questionnaire on a 'greater understanding of youth' (the fourth key plank of the European Union White Paper on youth, pursued through the 'Open Method of Co-ordination'), noted that:

> "A coherent strategy and work programme will be achieved with the process of drafted [sic] a national youth policy report and the formulation of a national youth policy in writing." (Cyprus Youth Board, response to European Commission questionnaire on 'Greater Understanding of Youth', p. 12)

Proposing relevant issues to the Commission for a study and research programme, the submission added:

> "Topic and priorities that are most relevant for such a strategy is [sic] the ones related to social cohesion, integration of young people to economic life (transition from full-time students to full-time employees), disadvantage[d] groups of young people and their integration to civil life, participation of young people in the decision-making processes, dissemination of quality information and equal access to information, gender equity to employment and political life, support of migrant and repatriated young people, safeguarding of the rights of young people to creative and artistic expression." (Cyprus Youth Board, response to European Commission questionnaire on 'Greater Understanding of Youth', p. 14)

One might assume that this is some kind of statement of the aspirations for youth policy in Cyprus, whether or not relevant strategic frameworks and operational programmes have yet been established.

In his welcome to the international review team on 1 June 2004, Mr Costas Papacostas, Member of the Cyprus Parliament and President of the House Standing Committee on Criminal Affairs, observed that:

> "It is with great pleasure that we have been informed that the Youth Board of Cyprus, in co-operation with the Council of Europe, the University of Cyprus and other public services and semi-government departments, are working together with the purpose of defining a National Youth Policy in Cyprus."

Likewise, the President of the Republic of Cyprus has been quite explicit that the Cyprus Government has among its aims 'to formulate a National Youth Policy that will deal in the long run with the needs and problems that the young generation is facing' and 'to take more account of youth and integrate youth policy in all government policies' (Governance Programme of Mr Tassos Papadopoulos, President of the Republic of Cyprus, p. 1). Priorities within this overarching aspiration were identified by the President as:

- The creative exploitation of leisure time
- The fields of culture and sports
- Juvenile delinquency and drugs
- Youth entrepreneurship
- Students
- Soldiers

One of the difficulties encountered, however, by the international review team was the presentation by different individuals and groups of rather different 'lists' of topics which merited priority attention in 'youth policy'. During brief presentations by the parliamentarians who were the chairs of different Parliamentary standing committees,[1] and the Parliamentary representative of the Maronite community, the following issues were identified:

- Drugs
- Unemployment (particularly among graduates)
- The involvement of young people in decision-making
- Tourism and globalisation – and its effect on Cypriot identity
- Young delinquents
- Refugees, missing persons and young people in enclaved areas
- Mobility
- Unification
- Violence in the family
- Education
- Gender equality
- Entrepreneurship and self-employment
- Europe – migration and return
- Multi-communal living and programmes
- Equal opportunities and human rights

Youth organisations came up with an equally long list, though with new topics and with different weight and focus attached to some of the issues already mentioned:

- Youth information and peer education
- Sexual health services
- Culture and education
- The environment
- Drugs and HIV/AIDS
- Health and eating disorders
- Participation and representation
- Parent education

---

1. The presentations covered: Human rights and education; Refugees, enclaved and missing persons; Crime, delinquency and drugs; Labour and social insurance; European Affairs.

- Academic pressures
- Military service
- The impact of the church
- Tourism and the sex industry
- The situation of Turkish Cypriot young people in the north – emigration and lack of access to European opportunities
- Crime
- Dangerous driving

As the international review team noted, these lists constituted a huge patchwork of issues and concerns. Many of these are already addressed to some degree in the extensive programmes organised through a variety of ministries[2] and captured within the Ministry of Finance Planning Bureau's National Development Plan for Youth Services between 2004 and 2006. This does not take account, in any detail, of the equally extensive work of the Cyprus Youth Board (though there is some overlap); that will be covered in more detail below.

What is clear, at this point, is the ambition, in its rhetoric and vision – and sometimes in its actuality – of services for young people in Cyprus. It is within the framework of this vision that the international review team hoped to make a productive contribution to a robust and transparent debate on the future shape and direction of youth policy in Cyprus. During the visits of the international review team, there was evidence of much forward-looking strategy and practice. These included, for example, the Youth Information Centres in Nicosia and Larnarca, the Anti-Drugs Council, and the ZEP school in Limassol – yet, equally, it is important to note that such developments were usually very new and it will be some time before their impact can be fully assessed.

The young people in Kato Pyrgos, an isolated community on the coast beyond the mountains and close to the closed border, also set out their aspirations for the components of 'youth policy'. In an animated and reflective discussion, they spoke enthusiastically of their international visits (many had travelled abroad), but also of the issues and concerns that affected them at home:

- The drugs culture
- Worries about their prospects for the future
- A sense of insecurity
- War and economic inequality
- Injustice
- The division of the island, a lack of communication with the north, and fears about more and more settlers coming to Cyprus
- A sense of disadvantage as a result of their geographical isolation

---

2. Ministry of Education and Culture: theatre organisation, health education, drugs education, environmental awareness, heritage, European programmes (Socrates), psychological support, prevention programmes, Zones of Education Priority, special education, counselling and guidance. Ministry of Interior: housing. Ministry of Labour: apprenticeship schemes, social welfare services, day care, hostels for juveniles, European programmes (Leonardo). Ministry of Commerce, Industry and Tourism: enterprise development. Ministry of Justice and Public Order: prisons, police department, Council for the Prevention and Combating of Delinquency, research programme. Ministry of Agriculture, Natural Resources and Environment: new farmers. Ministry of Defence: computer learning for young people doing military service. Ministry of Finance: state scholarships.

These young people felt that the recent accession of Cyprus to the European Union both extended opportunities to study abroad (and to do so more cheaply!) and conferred a greater sense of safety and security in relation to the Cyprus Problem. However, it was interesting that they felt the main reason for joining the EU was to solve the Cyprus Problem – something which, of course, was not achieved in tandem with that process. Indeed, various opinion polls following the rejection of the Annan Plan suggested that young Cypriots (both Greek and Turkish) were more opposed to this proposed settlement than other segments of the population. They were more inclined towards permanent separation of the two communities as a solution, though of course various interpretations can be placed upon such 'findings' (draft National Report, Culture chapter, p. 14). There are indeed counter-positions:

> "It is encouraging to observe today that the traumas of the island's painful and often bloodstained history, fraught with fatalities, disappearances, suffering and anguish, do not only provoke anger and bitterness but also – increasingly moreover – a yearning to press onward and look ahead to the future. Although the visit took place a few weeks after the failure of the plan for reunification put forward by UN Secretary General Kofi Annan, I gained the impression – particularly in my talks with the representatives of civil society on both sides of the island – that past misfortunes could be transformed into a unifying factor for the new generation. I noted with great satisfaction that the concept of human rights was no longer permeated by past bloodshed but embraced the emerging new realities and the new challenges taking shape in Cyprus." (Report by Mr Alvaro Gil-Robles, Commissioner for Human Rights, on his visit to Cyprus, 25-29 June 2003, Strasbourg, 12 February 2004, p. 3)

Later in his report, Mr Gil-Robles went on to comment that 'only in a framework of unrestricted democratic dialogue can the path of compromise be found' (p. 14). The international review team encountered diverse perspectives on the part of young people, some of which were certainly 'trapped' within required party political lines (for one striking feature of Cypriot youth is its strong political affiliations), but much of which was open, honest and forthright.

Recommendation 1:

The international review team endorses the need for an 'unrestricted democratic dialogue' among young people, to determine their perspectives on the Cyprus Problem.

Notwithstanding this overriding political framework, the international review team was interested in and concerned about all young people in Cyprus, irrespective of their geographical location, ethnicity or nationality. The living conditions, lifestyles, social circumstances, beliefs and aspirations of young people throughout Cyprus were our starting point – though we quickly discovered many difficulties in securing reliable information beyond that which pertained to the Greek Cypriot community. Nevertheless, the international review team sought to understand the context of young people's lives, the provision and opportunity available to them, and the problematics and challenges they faced.

In keeping with the legally prescribed framework for the Cyprus Youth Board, the international review team endeavoured to retain a focus on 'the progress and welfare of all the young people of Cyprus regardless of national origin or religion' (The

Youth Board Law, para. 6(a), p. 3). Indeed, in the Youth Board's budget for 2004, under Entry 711 for Youth and Sports, it proposed an 'Olympic Truce' initiative:

> "In 2004 Greece will host the Olympic Games. The Olympic Games promote the idea of Peace, Progress and Prosperity, Solidarity, Co-operation and Conciliation among Peoples.
>
> Given the fact that the Republic of Cyprus has signed the Olympic Truce Treaty (at the 6th Meeting of European Youth Ministers of the Council of Europe, in Thessaloniki, November 2002) and that our country remains divided, the Cyprus problem unsolved and the Green Line still presenting a serious threat for the future of Cyprus Youth, it was decided to proceed to a campaign promoting the idea of the truce and peace through the Olympic Games.
>
> For this purpose and in order to promote the above idea, the campaign will include the organisation of cultural events of a sports nature." (Budget 2004, pp. 31-2)

The Youth Board's own vision has been depicted as follows:

> "The young people of Cyprus want to live in a country, which is socially fair, democratic and free. In this country young people should have an upgraded social role through the ability to participate in the decision-making for youth-related matters." (Governing Board of the Cyprus Youth Board, Strategy Plan for the Directions of the 1999-2003 Five-Year Period, June 1998, p. 12)

The international review team would concur wholeheartedly with such a vision.

1. Council of Europe international reviews of national youth policy — a background

The Youth Directorate of the Council of Europe embarked on its international reviews of national youth policy in 1997. Finland was the first country to put itself forward for such a review, following by the Netherlands, Sweden, Romania, Spain, Estonia, Luxembourg, Lithuania, Malta and Norway. Cyprus is the eleventh country to be reviewed in this way. After the first seven such international reviews, a 'synthesis report' was written, comparing and contrasting the experiences and approaches of very different national contexts (see Williamson 2002).

The approach to the reviews has evolved over time, but they continue to have a triple purpose:

- To provide a critical reflection on youth policy development in the country concerned
- To provide ideas from the country concerned to inform youth policy development in other countries in Europe
- To provide material for an overarching framework for youth policy development across Europe

Why 'youth policy'? The answer is not a simple one, but derives from a growing body of academic research which suggests that the transitions of young people to adult life and citizenship have become increasingly challenging. They are now more complex, extended and non-linear; and new opportunities for many young people in the wider Europe have also produced corresponding vulnerability and risk. And whereas, in the past, the major preoccupation around 'youth transitions' related to pathways from school to work, the purview of 'youth policy' now needs to address questions not only of education and employment, but also health, housing, justice and family life. Indeed, the inclusion of the 'family' as one focus of youth policy has now led to a consideration of the need for a more integrated approach to childhood, youth and family policy.

This notwithstanding, policies affecting and directed at young people now have to accommodate the issues facing both adolescents and young adults. As a result, youth policy not only extends across a range of policy domains but also across a considerable age range. And though different countries have different ideas of 'youth', it is clear there is a general consensus about the terrain on which youth policy needs to be constructed: from the early teenage years well into young adulthood. Moreover, the ideal is to construct such a policy in an 'opportunity-focused', rather than 'a problem-orientated' way — opening up possibilities for positive choices and experiences, not simply seeking to 'troubleshoot' the problems caused and experienced by young people as they arise. Many young people do, of course, secure access to such positive pathways to adulthood through their own initiative and through the support of their families and neighbourhoods. Some, however, do not, and it is towards these young people that public policy interventions need to be more emphatically directed.

The Council of Europe's international reviews are now part of a wider framework of interest and commitment to the shaping and framing of 'youth policy'. The Youth Directorate engages in 'advisory missions': more fleeting visits to countries, to reflect on specific matters of concern. The essential distinction is that, whereas the international reviews are in the public domain, an advisory mission remains confidential to the country concerned. The Youth Directorate has also produced a report on 'youth policy indicators' (Council of Europe 2003a), outlining the objectives of youth policy and various measures by which its impact may be judged. There is also the EU White Paper on Youth Policy (European Commission 2001). This, through an Open Method of Co-ordination, has sought to disseminate good practice throughout the European Union on topics such as the participation of young people, youth information, voluntary activities and a greater understanding of youth (research). On the first of these topics, the Committee of Local and Regional Authorities of the Council of Europe has recently revised and approved a resolution on the participation of young people in local and regional life, which was first established under the Llangollen Declaration in 1992. (The European Youth Forum has produced a 'plain English' version of the new document!)

Cyprus is the second Mediterranean country to be the focus of an international review, after Malta, which was reviewed in 2003 (see Evans 2003). As well as Cyprus's historical position as a bridge between continents and cultures, it has since May 2004 acted as a bridge between the European Union and the wider world. Inevitably this has some negative implications (notably questions of migrants, drugs and trafficking in women) as well as many opportunities to give to and take from the wider Europe. Cyprus, like anywhere else, has its own distinctive traditions, from which it can contribute to the enlarged Europe but, as it undergoes the inevitable changes arising from multiculturalism and globalisation, it can also draw on the experience and traditions within that wider Europe.

The international review teams have generally been composed of three youth researchers (including the rapporteur) and a member of the Advisory Council of the Youth Directorate (a representative from a European youth NGO). The chair is drawn from the Council of Europe's inter-governmental steering committee on youth (the CDEJ) and the secretariat is provided by the Youth Directorate. Such arrangements are not, however, carved in stone. There is flexibility according to the specific issues and requirements of the country under review, something which is explored and established during a preliminary visit,[3] when a provisional programme is constructed for the team's first visit. Routinely, an international team makes two visits to the country concerned. The first is, typically, focused on 'top-down' issues –

3. Given the specific context and concerns of Cyprus, specialists on drug misuse and conflict resolution were included in the international review team. The team had, exceptionally, seven members, though the Chair for the first visit was unable to attend the second visit, and the drugs expert was unable to participate in the first visit. The team was Daniel Menschaert (CDEJ), Peter Lauritzen (Youth Directorate), Anca Sirbu (Advisory Council), Yael Ohana (Youth Directorate), Ditta Dolejsiova (Slovakia/Netherlands), Stanko Salamon (Slovenia) and Howard Williamson (UK).

through meetings with parliamentarians and ministries, when strategy and structure are explored. The second visit is more grounded and 'bottom-up' – through meetings with those who deliver provision and practice.

The 'synthesis report' of the first seven international reviews (Williamson 2002) suggested a framework for addressing 'youth policy', in relation both to discrete policy domains (such as education, health or housing) and to cross-cutting issues (such as multiculturalism and equal opportunities). This framework now provides a guide for the inquiry of the international review and a structure for presenting the final report of the international review team. Moreover, the 'synthesis report' put forward five 'C's (coverage, capacity, competence, co-ordination and cost) and four 'D's (drive, delivery, debate and development) for reflecting on youth policy. These, together with elements of the 'report on indicators' (Council of Europe 2003a) and guidelines for the formulation and implementation of youth policies (Council of Europe 2003b), inform the conclusions of the international review.

Most international review teams have had the benefit of a national report prior to embarking on their task. This was not the case in Cyprus (though nor was it in Lithuania or Norway). The Republic of Cyprus Government, through the Cyprus Youth Board, had requested the University of Cyprus to prepare a national youth report. Its content, however, was in embryonic form at the time of the first visit of the international review team, and still only in draft form at the time of our second visit. This report contains chapters on education, employment, health, justice and culture, as well as a 'scene-setting' chapter, conclusions and recommendations. Different governments have, admittedly, adopted different approaches to compiling a national report, though it is unusual for this to be placed so firmly and exclusively in the hands of an academic team.

In the absence of a comprehensive national youth policy report, the international review team had to gather data, where possible, from other sources. This accentuated a typical challenge for any such team: trying to judge whether it is 'chasing phantoms' or pursuing 'legitimate concerns'. Inevitably, a team's composition not only reflects the qualities and expertise identified by the country concerned (see above), but also projects the interests and commitments of its constituent members. Maintaining an appropriate balance between the two can sometimes be difficult without the anchor of a national youth policy report, which has been given a stamp of approval by the government concerned. Nonetheless, the international review team endeavoured to maintain this balance, through regular 'time-out' for consultation, clarification and discussion with members of the Administrative Board of the Cyprus Youth Board and, in particular, with its Executive Secretary and others of his professional colleagues.

The international review team, like its predecessors in relation to other countries, was keen to establish a 'communicative methodology' from a position of 'critical complicity'. In other words, it was insistent that it was not in the business of 'rubber-stamping' prevailing perspectives and practice. However, it was in the business of 'building something together' – taking the current work of the Cyprus Youth Board as a starting point but subjecting it, where possible, to a constructively critical interrogation.

2. introduction to Cyprus — the "nation" in question

In the context of Cyprus, deliberations on the subject of a national youth policy immediately beg the question of what 'nation' is meant. Since the invasion by Turkey in 1974, the island of Cyprus has been divided, with one-third of its land occupied by Turkey and designated, despite a lack of recognition by the rest of the world, as the Turkish Republic of Northern Cyprus. Despite the whole of the island joining the European Union in May 2004, the *acquis communautaire* remains suspended in the occupied north and a so-called 'Green Line' continues to run across the country, though passage through some checkpoints across the UN-controlled demilitarised zone has eased since the early part of 2003. (Indeed, some 30 000 Turkish Cypriots cross daily from north to south in Nicosia.)

Yet just five years after the Turkish invasion, talks were in progress about resolving the 'Cyprus problem':

> "It was agreed to abstain from any action which might jeopardise the outcome of the talks, and special importance will be given to initial practical measures by both sides to promote goodwill, mutual confidence and the return to normal conditions." (Republic of Cyprus Press and Information Office, The 10-Point Agreement of 19 May 1979, p. 1)

Regrettably, the question remains unresolved at the beginning of 2005.

Cyprus became an independent republic on 16 August 1960. However, its constitution, which incorporated a system of entrenched minority rights unparalleled in any other country, soon produced a constitutional deadlock. In July 1974, when the ruling military junta of Greece staged a coup to overthrow the democratically elected Government of Cyprus, Turkey invaded the north of the island, displacing about 142 000 Greek Cypriots (one quarter of the whole population and 80% of those living in the north). Those of the Turkish Cypriot minority (no more than 20% of the population of the whole island) who lived in the south fled to the north. Since 1974, the Turkish Cypriot population in the north has diminished, though the north of the island (unilaterally declared an independent 'state' in 1983) has been recurrently re-populated with Turkish settlers, largely from Anatolia in Turkey.

In July 2004, the population of Cyprus was estimated at 775 927, of whom 15.5% were aged 15-24. Of those aged 20 and over, 43% had completed secondary education and 25% had finished tertiary education. Almost three-quarters of the population lived in urban areas. Foreigners, including those working legally in Cyprus, comprised 10.5% of the population (though a similar number are thought to be working illegally in Cyprus), and unemployment was 3% (draft National Report, Crime chapter, p. 2). The population in northern Cyprus was estimated at 203 100 – 29% of the Greek Cypriot population in the areas controlled by the Republic of Cyprus – of whom 87 600 were Turkish Cypriots and 115 500 were settlers from Turkey (ibid., p. 5).

These are confident demographic data, but they may still need to be treated with some caution. Prior to independence in 1960, the ratio of Greek Cypriots to Turkish Cypriots was roughly 80:20, but it has been more difficult to be accurate since then.[4] In other documentary material consulted, it was argued that "it is practically impossible to obtain any figures of the island's total population after partition in July 1974, as censuses have been replaced by estimates" (Parliamentary Assembly of the Council of Europe, "The Demographic Structure of Cyprus 1992", para. 37). Figures for the Greek Cypriot population include the Maronite, Armenian and Latin Christian minorities (or more strictly "minor religious groups") who had opted for membership of the Greek Cypriot community, as they were allowed to do under the constitution.

It is, indeed, extremely difficult to garner reliable data in relation to the occupied north of the island, for its status as a self-proclaimed independent republic is not recognised by the international community:

> "The island's divided state resulting from the occupation of the northern part since 1974 and from the proclamation of the 'Turkish Republic of Northern Cyprus' ('TRNC') is familiar. The international community has condemned this development and in 1983 the United Nations Security Council adopted Resolution 541 (1983) declaring the proclamation of the 'TRNC' legally void." (Report by Mr Alvaro Gil-Robles, Commissioner for Human Rights, on his visit to Cyprus 25-29 June 2003, Strasbourg 12 February 2004, para. 45)

One figure that is recorded, however, is the significant disparity in the levels of economic development of the two parts of the island. Per capita income is some three times higher in the south. Linked to the economic question and the political challenge has been the steady influx of settlers from Turkey, which is seen in the south as a provocative and calculated attempt to manipulate the demographic structure of the island, though defended in the north in terms of a need to respond to economic needs. There is apparently a differential response on the part of Turkish Cypriots towards the increasing number of settlers. It is recorded that "there was no solidarity between the Turkish Cypriots and the settlers and some ethnic incidents had even been recorded" (Parliamentary Assembly of the Council of Europe, "The Demographic Structure of Cyprus 1992", para. 85).

---

4. The international review team received papers giving somewhat different figures. For example, in the response of Cyprus to the EU youth White Paper's consultation on youth participation, the total population of Cyprus is 671 300 (given data do not include the area occupied by Turkish troops). The percentage of the population aged 15-25 is about 14.2% (Cyprus Youth Board, European Commission Questionnaire on 'Participation', p. 1). In the Health chapter of the draft National Report, it is stated that 'The population of Cyprus is 793 100. Of these, 639 500 (80.7%) belong in the Greek-Cypriot community, 87 600 (11.0%) in the Turkish-Cypriot community and 66 000 are foreigners living in Cyprus' (draft National Report, Health chapter, p. 1). The health report goes on to say that 22.6% of the population are aged 15-29. Some data include figures from the northern part of Cyprus, but usually only for Turkish Cypriots, not for the settler population or the occupying troops.

The international review team grappled with this complexity, acknowledging the multiplicity of factors that have led to the sustaining of divisions and hostilities (which also include the treatment of Greek Cypriots in the enclaved areas of the north, and the destruction of antiquities), though it was unclear how it could respond to them in its report. It was, however, welcome to be reminded of the fact that, in the relatively recent past, Greek and Turkish Cypriots were living together harmoniously 'at the ground level'. One respondent made the point that this had been "quite normal" and emphasised that "the divisions are quite new, and the challenge is to see how the people can go back to living together within a common political framework – these issues are vital and crucial, especially for the youth".

Membership of the European Union was seen by many as "holding some promise in resolving the problem". It was often conceded that a solution was never going to be easy, because of sustaining antagonisms and rivalries, but it was suggested that now the dynamics are different, because the EU is essentially an integration process, which Cyprus could no longer ignore. Although accession to the EU had not been contingent, under any circumstances, upon a resolution to the Cyprus Problem, there was certainly a view that "the commencement of accession negotiations in early 1998 and the accession itself will be beneficial for both communities on the island and will help to speed up a peaceful solution in Cyprus" (Press and Information Office, "The EU-Cyprus Joint Parliamentary Committee Recommendation", p. 2). Both Greek Cypriot and Turkish Cypriot youth organisations, meeting as the Bi-Communal Youth Forum in Budapest in March 2002, certainly expressed the hope that "accomplishing a solution and accession to the EU at the same time will be the most ideal outcome" (Bi-Communal Youth Forum, Common Declaration 30 March 2002, para. 2). The Common Declaration went on to:

> "Realise that when a solution is established, the multicultural character, tradition, political culture, institutions and principles of human rights of the EU will serve for the integration and co-existence of the people of Cyprus in both communities." (ibid., para. 4)

There was clearly a perspective emanating from many quarters that the Cyprus Problem served to stifle debate on a range of 'modern' problems affecting young people in Cyprus and on the place of Cyprus within Europe and the international community. In a relatively short time, the island has travelled a long road – from decolonisation and independence, inter-communal conflict, the events that led to the occupation of the north of the island, making hundreds of thousands of people into refugees, the de facto partition for thirty years and now membership of the European Union. Over those fifty years there has been a constant tension between tradition and change: relating the authority of traditional institutions of the family and the church to growing levels of tourism and immigration.

The international review team had a sharp learning curve on two important fronts. Firstly, it heard constant historical and contemporary references to Cyprus as a bridge – or as a door to the west and a window to the east. The metaphor of the bridge is constantly invoked, and was indeed so by the President of the Republic of Cyprus shortly before accession to the EU:

> "As one of the external borders of the Union, Cyprus can become an economic, political and cultural bridge linking the two shores of the Mediterranean – a necessary bridge of mutual understanding and co-operation between the var-

ious religions, cultures and ways of life." (quoted in draft National Report, Culture chapter, p. 19)

Yet the international review team had necessarily to ask itself how Cyprus could continue to proclaim this function, when it has manifestly failed to bridge its own divide. Secondly, that very challenge was differently depicted as a 'question', a 'problem', an 'issue' or indeed a 'tragedy'. In relation to young people, the international review team came to see it more as a conundrum, for it was repeatedly apparent that professional desire for change at ground level was paralysed and contained by political entrenchment, yet political positions were unlikely to shift until there was some movement on the ground. Part of the work of the international review team was therefore – in relation to the lives of young people in Cyprus – to itself act as a bridge between the political decision-makers in the field of youth policy and the professionals striving to broaden opportunity structures in the daily lives of young people.

The meetings held during the two visits of the international review team were the start of this process, through an information exchange which appraised the team of the traditions, culture and social condition of young people in Cyprus and informed those the team spoke to of principles and practice that prevail elsewhere in Europe. It is to be hoped that those kernels of dialogue can be developed further – in, for example, seminars and training sessions, through the reflections of this report.

3. Youth and youth policy in Cyprus

3.1. Youth defined

Different countries have different conceptions of 'youth'. Its parameters are usually, though not always, defined by age, but the age range differs enormously. Malaysia is often cited for defining 'youth' as extending to the age of 40. Within the Soviet Union and its satellites, 'youth' extended to 29, whereas in western Europe until recently 'youth' was normally considered to be the teenage years, up to the age of 19. Now, it is more likely to be thought of as extending to the age of 25. Not that the upper limits of 'youth' are simply defined by age; it is also contextualised by, for example, the typical duration of the retention of young people in education or the average age for leaving 'home' (usually meaning the family of origin).

Age-based criteria for youth have to determine not only an 'upper limit', but also a starting point – the 'transition' point between 'childhood' and 'youth'. This is equally problematic, for it is quite clear that there is an increasing overlap between these two concepts: 'youth' now extends further downwards as children are subjected to forces of consumption that previously were directed at young people, while young people often remain more dependent, like children, for a longer period – what Jones and Wallace (1992) called 'quasi-citizenship'. Moreover, the framework within which 'youth' is defined is strongly framed in some countries and weakly framed in others. And, even when the concept appears to be strongly framed, there are usually very different points at which, for example, individuals may leave school, be considered responsible for criminal behaviour, purchase alcohol or drive a car. Thus there is no universally agreed idea of 'youth', but it is clearly necessary to have some sense of the concept if a 'youth policy' is to be constructed.

Cyprus appears to have a relatively weakly specified definition of youth, though this is not a criticism. It is simply to note that there seems to be a fluidity in understanding the 'idea' of young people. Young people in Cyprus remain more closely attached to their families and communities until the moment arises for them to depart; in this sense, in comparison to young people elsewhere in Europe, they 'drift' into adulthood, having completed what is often a protracted education and eventually found a position in the labour market. This suggests an upper limit to 'youth' somewhere between 25 and 30. At the other end of the spectrum, when one examines the provision supported by the Cyprus Youth Board, it is clear that the idea of youth often extends downwards to the start of secondary schooling (age 11). This inevitably produces an overlap between 'childhood' and 'youth', for the UN Convention on the Rights of the Child relates to those up to the age of 18. It was argued elsewhere that 'youth' in Cyprus should include 12- to 25-year-olds, though it was noted that age 16 is the threshold of adulthood in relation to criminal juris-diction (draft National Report, Crime chapter, p. 2). This notwithstanding, the inter-national review team accepted a working definition of 'youth' in Cyprus as those between the ages of 10 and 25 – the period of secondary and tertiary education.

Recommendation 2:

Given the de facto age range addressed under the banner of 'youth', consideration should be given to re-naming the Cyprus Youth Board as the Cyprus Children and Youth Board – which reflects more accurately its frame of reference.

3.2. Youth policy defined

'Youth policy' is an equally contested concept, which in the past was often held to cover little more than 'youth work' policy. Its range and depth remains a matter for debate, but what is not now contested is that all countries have a youth policy – in the sense that they have policies (or an absence of policies) that affect the quality and direction of young people's lives. What is more, such policies can work in har-mony or in conflict with each other, and they can be either proactive (in creating positive conditions for young people to live their lives) or reactive to emergent prob-lems caused or experienced by young people. The essential point about a 'youth policy' discussion is to consider the coherence (integration) and purposefulness of state and NGO activity directed at young people – both in relation to what is being done and what perhaps should be done.

In this respect, any policies touching the lives of young people are part of 'youth policy': obviously education, training and labour market measures, but also provi-sion for leisure, criminal justice frameworks and, indeed, requirements for military service. Family policy and child welfare also impinge on youth policy, for it has both generalist/universal components (such as compulsory schooling) and specialist/selective elements directed at particular groups of young people, according to their needs, vulnerabilities or problematics. And, in order to determine how such issues should be addressed and the priority that should be attached to particular issues, 'youth policy' needs to be guided, though not governed, by the findings and analysis of youth research. In this way, the shape and direction of youth policy is established, and relevant and meaningful provision and practice are put in place.

The international review team noted from the very start the often quite impressive range of practice being developed in Cyprus, significantly under the auspices (or with the financial support) of the Cyprus Youth Board. Yet the team found it difficult to distil a clear formulation or rationale for these developments within any overall concept of 'youth policy'. It has been noted that the international review team was presented with many 'lists' of key issues and challenges facing young people in Cyprus, but these were never 'packaged' within an over-arching strategy. It is not for the international review team to prescribe what such a strategy (or strategies – there will probably be more than one) should be, but elsewhere in Europe some such approaches have been concerned with 'active citizenship', 'social inclusion' or 'lifelong learning'. Given the specificities of Cyprus, there might be important themes of 'multiculturalism' or 'internationalism'.

> **Recommendation 3:**
>
> The vision for 'youth policy' in Cyprus needs to be more firmly delineated, identifying the guiding and governing themes within which the range of operational activity can be located.

The international review team acknowledges that 'youth policy' in Cyprus is in a relatively early stage of development. Responsibility for its formulation and implementation will rest heavily on the Cyprus Youth Board, about which we will comment in more detail later. Here it is sufficient to say that the international review team felt that the idea of 'youth policy' needed to be 'pinned down', and the place of both research and civil society in contributing to it more firmly articulated.

3.3. The Cyprus Youth Board

The Youth Board itself conveniently displays an ambiguity in its position – sometimes it is an NGO, sometimes the government. Each position carries strengths and weaknesses, and we hope that the advantages of each can be exploited. Equally, however, the disadvantages of each may become more prominent, leaving the development and execution of a robust and purposeful youth policy in a vacuum. From a very different policy context (Australia), the international review team was reminded of a critical question: [Is the Cyprus Youth Board] the head of a movement or an arm of the state? One senior official expressed disappointment that many critical youth (policy) issues were not being discussed because they were submerged within the Cyprus Problem. Another noted, however, that the constitution of the Cyprus Youth Board (see below) already represented about 95% of the youth population of Cyprus 'and so no big group [of young people] is not represented on the Board'.

The Cyprus Youth Board is the key driver of youth policy in Cyprus. To do this effectively, the international review team feels that the board needs to consolidate and strengthen its relations with youth research and youth NGOs, the other partners in what has come to be known as the 'triangle' – the critical elements required for the effective development and delivery of youth policy and practice.

3.3.1. Legislation

In its response to the EU youth White Paper questionnaire on youth participation, the Youth Board wrote:

> "There is no specific legislation covering all youth affairs. However, special legislative provisions covering young people exist in a number of laws.
>
> The Youth Board of Cyprus Law No. 33(1)/94 is administered, by the Administrative Board, appointed by the Council of Ministers and consists of the President, the Vice-President and five members ....
>
> As a semi-governmental organisation, independent from the civil service, [the Cyprus Youth Board] promotes the active participation of youth, in the social economic and cultural development of the country. Specifically it is mentioned in the Law of the Youth Board, that one of the Objects of the Board is the granting of equal opportunities to all young people and the relevant organisa-

tions for participation and assumption of responsibility in the social, economic and cultural development and progress of their community and the country in general.

The aim of the government policy in the Youth Sector is to provide children and young people [with] equal opportunities and treatment and to promote and encourage their personal development.

Specific objectives of the Youth Policy include the following: to encourage young people to participate in the affairs of the country (in its economic life and in the decision-making process), – to ensure that young people will have the education and training for their integration into the economic life of the country, – to support young couples in acquiring their own home, – to support young people in setting up their own business, – to run programmes like Youth Clubs mainly in rural areas, Youth Card, etc., – to set up Youth Information Centres, and – to encourage the establishment of Youth Exchange Programmes.

The Youth Board of Cyprus can submit proposals to the government concerning the formulation of policies on youth matters. It can also initiate new programmes and implement them in areas that are not covered by other departments." (Cyprus Youth Board response to EU Youth White Paper questionnaire on participation, pp. 4-5)

The over-riding object of the Cyprus Youth Board is to "advise, through the Minister [of Justice], the Council of Ministers, about the shaping of a comprehensive and specialised policy on youth matters" (The Youth Board Law, p. 3).

The Cyprus Youth Board, which succeeded the Central Youth Agency, was established through a unanimous vote in the House of Representatives in April 1994, and its first Governing Board (Administrative Board) was appointed in June 1994.

3.3.2. Budget and finance

Despite the considerable fiscal deficit and strong pressures on public expenditure in Cyprus (through significant public sector employment and the military demands for defence), budget allocations to the Cyprus Youth Board – through which the bulk of youth policy activity is channelled – are generous. The Central Youth Agency (1990-3) received a diminishing budget and its initial allocation in 1990 of 552 575 Cyprus pounds (CYP)[5] was achieved by the Cyprus Youth Board only in 1997 (Governing Board of the Cyprus Youth Board, Strategic Plan for the Directions of the 1999-2003 Five-Year Period, June 1998, Appendix B). Since then, however, the budget has increased steadily; the budget for 2004 being, in total, 2 759 350 CYP, though some of this was secured through external funding, the private sector and international sponsorship, including the European Union (which contributed 322 132 CYP in 2004 for implementation of the 'YOUTH' programme, which Cyprus joined in 2001. These resources are directed at a range of disparate initiatives, including:

- youth clubs (buildings and running costs, staffing and coaches),
- international relations,

---

5. The Cyprus pound is approximately equivalent to 1.7 Euro [€].

- the healthy and creative occupation of young people (culture, art and play; multi-functional youth centres; youth information centres; youth festivals and youth camps; Youth Card; subsidies to youth organisations; information services on substance misuse and HIV/AIDS; new technologies; sporting activities; municipal youth councils; youth research; conferences and seminars; specialised programmes and campaigns – including voluntary activities and environmental issues; support for Cypriot youth overseas; bi-communal activities; youth parliament),

- the European YOUTH programme, and

- National Service administrative expenses.

As in most countries, however, it is not possible to determine precise figures for expenditure on 'youth policy', even if in Cyprus the work of the Youth Board is the main conduit for its delivery. For example, solely in the area of youth volunteering (voluntary activities) – and beyond the very real problematic of defining exactly what that is – resources are not simply channelled through the Youth Board. The Youth Board does contribute some 9 000 CYP "exclusively for the funding of voluntary activities of various youth groups and for the realisation of activities that aim at promoting the value of volunteering among the Cyprus youth" (Cyprus Youth Board response to EU Youth White Paper questionnaire on voluntary activities, pp. 2-3). There is also 5 000 Euros available for the hosting of up to three young foreigners in Cyprus, under the European Voluntary Service (EVS) programme. However, beyond these dedicated resources, the Republic of Cyprus Government makes available some 3 900 000 CYP to support the work of NGOs engaging in voluntary activities (which, presumably, involves a proportion of young people), and the Ministry of Labour supports the work of the Pan-Cyprian Welfare Council "which then distributes to its member organisations for the purposes of assisting their operations" (ibid., p. 3). For these reasons, it is therefore "not possible to estimate the exact amount that is annually available for organising and holding voluntary activities" (ibid., p. 3).

Beyond these more peripheral, though very important, allocations to the lives and opportunities of young people, the budget of the Cyprus Youth Board is without doubt the important engine for the development of 'youth policy' in Cyprus. That it has steadily increased (through proposals by the Governing/Administrative Board and subsequent approval by Parliament) reflects political commitment to young people and the importance the state attaches to the idea of youth policy. Where other ministries take the lead and allocate resources in different domains of youth policy, the international review team was told that it is still the Cyprus Youth Board which ensures they "discharge their obligations".

3.3.3. Structures for delivery

The Cyprus Youth Board is now in the fourth phase of what have been called 'creation cycles': the first (1990-3) was the period of the Central Youth Agency; the second (1994-8) witnessed the establishment of the Cyprus Youth Board; the third (1999-2003) included 'the preparation of a study/proposal, to be given to the Government, on a single policy for youth with(in) the provisions of the Youth Board Law (Governing Board of the Cyprus Youth Board, Strategic Plan for the Directions of the 1999-2003 Five-Year Period, para. 4B.f.). The Cyprus Youth Board has been considered to be developmental and innovative, drawing ideas and lessons from across Europe and implementing a range of programmes and initiatives.

The governance of the Cyprus Youth Board is complex, with a range of actors, and is proclaimed as being premised upon a philosophy of 'co-management'. Some, however, would disagree, and there are clearly tensions between its 'directorial' approach and its more 'participative' practice. Indeed, by virtue of the law that established the board, it has two roles: an advisory and co-ordinating role in government, for policy issues relating to youth, and an executive role for programmes and policy implemented by the board itself.

The international review team heard, from a range of quarters, that the board should be more active in exercising the first role – by challenging the government, rather than primarily delivering initiatives that have been approved by government. Such challenges may not be so easy, especially given that the pivotal authority of the Youth Board – its Administrative Board – is composed of seven individuals from the youth wings of political parties. Indeed, four are nominated by the four largest political parties in Parliament (and then appointed by the Council of Ministers), while the remaining three (including the Chair/President and Vice-Chair/Vice-President) are appointed directly by the Council of Ministers.

The work of the Administrative Board is informed by three advisory committees: a Political Youth Committee, a Trade Union Advisory Body (the youth bodies of the Workers' and Farmers' coalitions), and a General Advisory Body. There is also a Students' Committee, representing high school, college and university student organisations. The General Advisory Body consists of the Political Committee, the Student Committee and the Trade Union Committee as well as some other non-aligned youth organisations – some 40 in total. The General Advisory Body is described differently in different documents, but is considered by the Cyprus Youth Board to be "an umbrella body for all the youth organisations that participate in the Youth Board's activities". The board is managed by an Executive Secretary. It is accountable to the Minister of Justice and Public Order (and in turn to the Council of Ministers, Parliament and the President of the Republic), though its work is also informed by a Consultative Intra-Departmental Committee spanning the ministries of the Republic of Cyprus Government.[6] Figure 1 is a flow-chart depicting these relationships.

Figure 1: The structure of the Cyprus Youth Board

President of Cyprus
Parliament
Council of Ministers
Minister of Justice and Public Order
Consultative Intra-Departmental Committee
Administrative Board

a. Political [Youth] Committee
b. Trade Union Body
c. [General] Advisory Body
d. Students' Committee

Executive Secretary
Staff of the Youth Board
[specific and area responsibilities]
Associates of the Youth Board

[bi-communal programme, youth clubs, youth information centres, drugs hotline]

6. The ministries of Justice and Public Order; Foreign Affairs; the Interior; Labour and Social Insurance; Finance; Transport; Health; Trade, Industry and Tourism; Education and Culture; Agriculture, Environment and Natural Resources; and Defence. Also, the Human Resources Development Authority.

Notwithstanding some criticism of the Cyprus Youth Board, it is generally widely acclaimed: "the social and cultural action of the Cyprus Youth Board has been tremendous" (draft National Report, Culture chapter, p. 24):

> "The youth look up to the Cyprus Youth Board as a forum that promotes youth issues and takes initiatives of social and cultural intervention towards fields of action where the government, due to bureaucratic difficulties, cultural inertia or ideological bias has failed to do so. Furthermore, the Board, according to NGOs and other youth organisations, has almost always been ready to assist several cultural initiatives whenever its aid, financial or organization [sic], was asked for." (ibid., p. 24)

These observations derived from focus-group interviews with members of youth organisations, university and college students, activists and respresentatives of ethnic-religious minorities in Cyprus. They are a powerful tribute to the work of the Cyprus Youth Board. It was argued further that the board has not only constructively exercised the flexibility and power conferred upon it, but has done so with political courage to address problems and promote initiatives that would otherwise have remained submerged in a 'culture of silence'. All this is a highly commendable testament to the board, and a far cry from the criticism (and sometimes self-criticism) that it remains too subject to political influence and fails to operate with sufficient participative democracy.

Such criticism must, however, be taken into account. The international review team was impressed that the Administrative Board, composed of political youth representatives from across the political spectrum, spoke with a collective commitment to youth issues. However, it was not completely comfortable with the criteria for their appointment nor wholly persuaded that it worked authentically on a system and process of 'co-management'.[7] On the criteria, the fact that the Administrative Board was composed solely of men (despite the counter-argument that this was merely coincidence) was a matter of some concern. On the question of co-management, a feeling was expressed in some quarters, and acknowledged by the international review team, that the Administrative Board took much more note of the Political Committee's views than those of the General Advisory Board.

Now that the Cyprus Youth Board has attained a level of maturity and recognition, it may be timely – at the start of this fourth 'creation cycle' – to consider broadening the composition of the decision-making Administrative Board in order to include, for example, two members from non-aligned youth organisations or from a 'minority' group. It should also set criteria for gender equality within its framework of governance. These might be considered contentious propositions, but their implementation would strengthen perceptions of the Cyprus Youth Board reflecting perspectives beyond the entrenched political establishment.

Recommendation 4:

The international review team believes that it would be timely for the Republic of Cyprus Government to consider amending the legal constitution of the Cyprus Youth Board in order to broaden the composition of its Governing/Administrative Board, to include representation beyond the established youth wings of the dominant political parties, and to set criteria for gender equality.

---

7. In 2004 the Cyprus Youth Board established a process of consultation on a range of youth issues. One issue was active participation in decision making. That working group maintained that at a national level "active participation of youth in the decision making process is not feasible through the Youth Board since only the Political Youth Parties are involved in the decision making process of the Youth Board" (Recommendations of the Working Group for Active Participation in Decision Making for the Cyprus Youth Policy, p. 15).

Nevertheless, the board has instituted a range of initiatives and sought to establish structures that can feed into its thinking from a more grounded perspective. It has developed an anti-drugs helpline and impressive Youth Information Centres in Nicosia and Larnarca, and supports a network of youth clubs, largely in rural areas. And, flowing from a commitment to the charter for participation in local and regional life, it has supported the emergence of municipal youth councils.

In its response to the EU Youth White Paper questionnaire on voluntary activities, the Cyprus Youth Board depicted the local provision it supported:

"At the local level, there are community and municipal youth councils, and the youth centres of each community. Youth Councils aim at representing young people in their local authorities and at promoting their participation in the decision making mechanisms of their area. Youth Centres aim at creating health a vocation for the youngsters, and at giving them numerous opportunities for recreation, and engagement in various cultural, educational, athletic activities …. A significant number of youth clubs also exists, that has as its priority to offer to youngsters opportunities for activities and extracurricular avocation." (Cyprus Youth Board response to EU youth White Paper on voluntary activities, p. 4)

This all sounds very commendable and the Cyprus Youth Board is intent on sustaining its support for municipal youth councils. In its budget outline for 2004, it recognises the "need for young people to be involved in local administration, and will [therefore] continue to promote and implement the institution in Cyprus (Budget 2004, p. 32). Yet the composition, role and function of the municipal youth councils has been subject to some criticism. They were first established in 2001 following discussion between the Cyprus Youth Board and the municipalities, and various protocols were agreed. One, for example, was that a municipal youth council would be chaired by a (preferably the youngest) member of the municipality council. This is symptomatic of the political control exercised over the youth councils, which clearly risks stifling their autonomy and independence, a risk that is evidently more pronounced when one looks at the detail of the arrangements for these councils:

"The operation of the Municipal Youth Councils is determined by internal regulations which are approved 'by the Municipal Authorities [elected through party nominations] after co-ordination with the organised youth bodies that have been active in the certain municipality... [T]he Municipal Youth Councils 'under no circumstances will substitute the organised youth bodies or act antagonistically to them'... 'They will develop action only in fields where the organised youth bodies fall short of doing so'" (draft National Report, Culture chapter, p. 34)

In so far as municipal youth councils were intended to broaden the active participation of young people in the life of their communities, they are eminently a development to be supported. The Cyprus Youth Board did convene a meeting in 2003 to explore the future of municipal youth councils, which generated some proposals for further development. More recently, in 2004, it has been suggested that these councils should elect their own chair, membership should be open to all youth NGOs working in the municipality, and that each member of a municipal youth council should participate in at least one of the municipality's committees (Recommendations of Working Group for Active Participation in Decision-Making for Cyprus Youth Policy, p. 17). In short, these and other proposals express a desire for the composition, role and function of municipal youth councils to be more clearly detached from local political control, in order to establish more robust civil society at the local level. This would be consistent with the Council of Europe's charter on youth participation at the local and regional level, which the Cyprus Youth Board maintains is an underpinning influence on the establishment and development of municipal youth councils.

Recommendation 5:

The international review team commends the initiative by the Cyprus Youth Board and the municipalities of Cyprus to establish municipal youth councils, but believes that these need to be based on greater autonomy and self-determination by youth NGOs and less constrained by the political framework which currently governs their existence.

Much the same argument applies to the development of youth clubs in rural areas. The Cyprus Youth Board has supported the establishment of nearly a hundred of these clubs, but it remains dependent on municipalities for the provision of buildings and approval of their programmes. These youth clubs cater for young people between the ages of 12 and 30 in localities where there is little else to do, and certainly no private provision. While some, subject to the staffing available, clearly offer a modern programme addressing contemporary needs and aspirations of young people, others "are burdened with an unspoken expectation to operate like museums of folklore culture, depositories of local morals and values, identity anchor and reference points for the diaspora" (draft National Report, Culture chapter, p. 34). Throughout Europe, when young people are consulted on their wishes for youth clubs and centres, they invariably come up with some version of the following four 'A's:[8]

- Association – somewhere to meet
- Activities – something to do
- Autonomy – space of our own
- Advice – someone to talk to

An effective response to these aspirations will require the sacrifice of some control by adults generally and the political establishment in particular. It will also demand a calibrated and professional approach on the part of 'youth workers' engaged with young people, in order that they balance a reactive and proactive stance in the development and delivery of a 'programme'. The next step, therefore, in the important initiative by the Cyprus Youth Board to set up a network of local youth clubs in areas where young people have access to little other provision, may be to 'professionalise' this service, through dialogue with local politicians (to secure a more 'arm's-length' position) and through a training programme for those adults (usually volunteers) who are committed to meeting the needs of local young people.

Recommendation 6:

The international review team applauds the development of a network of local youth clubs and centres, but believes these should be more firmly detached from local political influence and control, and that those who provide the programme of activities should have access to local-level training courses equipping them with the knowledge and skills of effective youth work.

---

8. See, for example, Williamson (1997), The Needs of Young People and the Youth Work Response, Caerphilly: Wales Youth Agency.

Youth and youth policy in Cyprus

Beyond the modest provision of local youth clubs and centres, the Cyprus Youth Board is in the process of supporting the development of what are called 'multi-functional youth centres'. A large centre is already proposed:

"The Centre's aim will be to approach young people, in a responsible and dynamic way, to support and promote initiatives and actions, aimed at upgrading their relationship with the state, their political emancipation and their active participation both in issues that concern them in particular broader issues that concern the society in which they live. In addition to being a meeting place and place of healthy occupation the Multifunctional Centre will also be a place of accommodation for a limited number of young people." (Budget 2004, p. 21)

This flagship centre, for which a location has already been identified, would also house a number of prominent youth organisations, and serve as the administrative offices for the Cyprus Youth Board.

Moreover, the Youth Board also proposes other such centres, which would be "a miniature version of the larger scale multifunctional youth centres" (Budget 2004, p. 29). This initiative found unconditional support in the draft National Report:

"Bearing in mind that the dominant local culture can be more asphyxiating for youth particularly in small, closed, rural communities, we find such cultural Polykentra are essential. They can create zones of safe speech and experimentation with new cultural activities and new ideas, but they can also operate as platforms for intra-European mobility. Imagine the energy of cultural literacy and mobility that rural Polykentra would spark if they also housed hostels for European students. Such Polykentra could function as depots of youth mobility to and from Europe. Excluded from programmes such as Erasmus, either due to their parents' mentality or due to the fact that they do not continue their studies in higher education (or if they do, they attend only programmes of study in private colleges and not at the University of Cyprus, the only higher education institution involved in the Erasmus programme), the rural youth would benefit enormously from opportunities to travel abroad." (draft National Report, Culture chapter, p. 35)

> **Recommendation 7:**
>
> The international review team commends the vision and ambition about such multifunctional centres. It acknowledges the considerable capital and revenue resources required for their development, but wholly supports the Cyprus Youth Board in its endeavour to secure the necessary funding.

Finally,[9] in terms of vertical delivery, there is the engagement with the European YOUTH programme, in which Cyprus has been involved since 2001 and to which the Cyprus Youth Board is strongly committed. It is also a programme in which young Cypriots appear to be very interested. The key issue here is equality of access for Greek and Turkish Cypriots. Theoretically, both have access to the programme, but there is, first, the question of access to information about the programme, and, secondly, the question of actual participation.

---

9. There are, of course, other areas of significant 'policy-to-practice' development established and supported by the Cyprus Youth Board. These include the Youth Information Centres in Nicosia and Larnarca, the anti-drugs council, the ZEP school in Limassol, and the Women's Information and Support Centre (in Apanemi – also in Limassol). All are impressive and pioneering initiatives. They will be considered elsewhere in this report.

During the visit of the international review team, when it heard various concerns expressed by young people from the Turkish Cypriot community, undertakings were made both to provide relevant information in the Turkish language and to locate an access point to the YOUTH programme on the Green Line at the checkpoint in Nicosia. The latter falls somewhat short of the request by Turkish Cypriot NGOs for a sub-branch of the national agency for the YOUTH programme to be established in the north of Cyprus, but clearly this is not a feasible option in the current circumstances.

Recommendation 8:

The international review team believes strongly that information concerning the European YOUTH programme should be made available in both the official languages of Cyprus: Greek and Turkish. It also wishes to support the undertaking to have a mobile information base positioned in the Green Line at the checkpoint in Nicosia, which may encourage and assist young Turkish Cypriots in securing more equal access to participation in the different elements of the YOUTH programme.

3.3.4. Partners and co-operation

"For the materialisation of [the vision and strategy of the Cyprus Youth Board], it is necessary to have co-operation among all agencies and powers of the State in all fields and in particular with the financial support of the Cyprus Youth Board." (Governing Board of the Cyprus Youth Board, Strategic Plan for the Directions of the 1999-2003 Five-Year Period, p. 12)

In any discussion of 'structures for delivery' of youth policy, it is necessary to consider not only the vertical structures discussed above, but also the horizontal structures at different levels of 'governance'. Wherever there may be a body designated to 'lead' on youth policy (as the Cyprus Youth Board clearly does in the case of Cyprus), that lead does not control all aspects of youth policy development and related policies that may affect young people. That is self-evident. What needs to be explored is the level of influence and potential for dialogue which such a 'lead' body has with other 'partners' in the youth policy enterprise. The Cyprus Youth Board is in a relatively strong position vis-à-vis similar 'national youth agencies' in other countries: it has a statutory mandate to 'advise', through the Ministry of Justice, across departments of government, and it can execute a range of self-determined programmes.

Moreover, at the level of government, its work is informed by a consultative intradepartmental committee comprising representatives of all government ministries. This, however, meets just once a year and, as one of those representatives told the international review team, "co-ordination is always a problem across departments". This view was echoed by other representatives on the committee, one of whom suggested that "each department tends to do its own bit on a particular issue – the issue it is responsible for", while another was forthright in their remark that:

"Speaking as a citizen, I have to say there is no overarching cross-sectoral approach. There must be a leader. Otherwise, if everybody does their own little part, then you never reach your objectives. Too much that we do is reflexive and reactionary. There needs to be a framework, strategy and process. We need to set more clear objectives across a range of issues and determine who is responsible for their achievement."

Such difficulties were attributed by another representative to the highly politicised culture of Cyprus: "people want immediate pay-offs, not any long-term rationale and evidence-based process and programme". The international review team was also told that the "rigidity" of Cypriot culture produced conservatism and caution on youth issues: "it is easy to go too far, beyond what the society will accept, in trying to solve the problems of young people".

Yet, despite such self-reflexive criticism, there is clearly counter-evidence of effective partnership development, steered professionally and purposefully by the Cyprus Youth Board. Other representatives on the intra-departmental committee acknowledged this, and felt that the committee itself was a useful vehicle for cross-fertilising strategic ideas and development: "I cannot emphasise enough the importance of ministries getting together, hearing what the agendas are in other ministries, and taking issues back to our own ministry". It was pointed out that the anti-drugs agenda demanded close co-operation between the police, health services and education (though the Cyprus Youth Board was quick to observe that this was the responsibility of the anti-drugs council, not the board, even though the board is a partner in this work). Indeed, another representative emphasised that there was a range of 'youth policies' within the overall strategic plan of the government: "the thing is the follow-up of the plan to keep track of the implementation of the targets … usually the only places these are discussed is during the annual budget round". (This comment raised questions in the mind of the international review team about 'performance monitoring' and 'quality assurance', though no answers were provided on this front.)

The Cyprus Youth Board is clearly perceived to be the central driver of 'youth policy' issues. Nevertheless, in its efforts to construct coherent and integrated strategy, it has to contend with the independent trajectories of different ministries, the representative of one of which described their approach as "we see a problem, its extent, then the need, and so then establish appropriate mechanisms for addressing it". It was not clear whether or not this necessarily involved prior consultation with the Youth Board. What was clear was that there was reticence about the idea of establishing an overarching youth policy on top of all ministries: "this could be very contentious". By and large, there was a view that the intra-departmental committee did engage with the key youth policy issues and that the Cyprus Youth Board was generally closely involved, across the spectrum, in this debate. There were, inevitably, problems about communication and co-ordination (an example was given of two ministries seeking to address the same 'problem' independently, in very different ways), but good foundations for improving this had been established.

The Cyprus Youth Board and its 'sponsor' department, the Ministry of Justice, concurred with this view:

"The process is becoming better and better every day. Sometimes it is still difficult, of course. Different ministries are still 'kingdoms', so communication is still a challenge. But problems and obstacles will be discussed and, if necessary, resolved at a higher level."

Those within the Youth Board conceded that there had been a time when there had been "problems about getting our voice heard", but the re-establishment of the intra-departmental committee had improved things significantly: "the Youth Board is increasingly invited to give a perspective to different sections of government". Indeed, one of the main objectives of 'youth policy' within the governance programme of Cyprus is for "the government programmes and policies that will be formulated and implemented [to] take into account their impact on youth and include provisions, which promote the role, progress and wellness of young people" (Governance Programme of Mr Tassos Papadopoulos, President of the Republic of Cyprus, p. 1).

At the municipal and local level, it was less clear that there was a great deal of structured cross-sectoral dialogue and communication, and co-ordinated practice. Not that this is unexpected, for it is a typical situation in many parts of Europe. However, there is increasing recognition that best practice requires some formalised arrangements at the local level. The international review team gained glimpses of such practice in Cyprus (notably in relation to the work of the ZEP school and Apanemi, the Women's Information and Support Centre, both in Limassol), but this seemed to derive significantly from the initiative and commitment of those concerned, rather than any more structured expectations. Indeed, the scathing allegation was made by one respondent that "in Cyprus, no-one takes the responsibility and each throws the responsibility on to another". The implication, corroborated by others with whom the international review team spoke, was that there remains a strong sense of professional 'territorialism': "there is too much focus on the content of the work, without more context-related consideration".

It is nevertheless evident that much of the delivery of youth policy depends – if it is to be effective and maximise its potential – on collaboration by a range of actors at local level. Rural youth clubs, for example, may have their running costs supported by the Cyprus Youth Board, but the provision they make rests on the consent of the local authority and support from the local community. Youth NGOs commented that they needed support 'in kind', if not through finance, from municipalities for such things as building use and accommodation.

There was a prevailing view that 'direction' was always awaited 'from the top': "if the ministry gives the green light, then it's okay". There is certainly no problem, in many respects, with the idea of strong political leadership from the centre, but the calibration of youth policy delivery so that it is responsive to local needs also requires a more grounded analysis and advocacy – drawing on lessons from the local context and having mechanisms for projecting those lessons into the national debate. That demands local forums in which the voices of those from different professional domains (for example, schooling, police, health or youth clubs) can be aired, shared and 'synthesised' so that local practice works in harmony and not in isolation or, at worst, in opposition.

3.4. Youth organisations

Youth organisations, it hardly needs saying, make an essential contribution to the formulation and development of effective youth policy. Not only is their involvement consistent with Article 12 of the United Nations Convention on the Rights of the Child (which asserts the right of the voice of children and young people to be heard), but it helps to make the practice of active citizenship possible and provides a 'reality check' on the quality and meaning of practice.

The international review team discovered that in Cyprus youth organisations tend to be 'highly politicised', many being youth wings of political parties and trade unions. "In order to exist as a youth in Cyprus, you have to be a political youth", was the comment of one young person (draft National Report, Culture chapter, p. 29). At youth organisational level, this also seems to be the prevailing view: political youth organisations are considered to hold sway, while other youth organisations feel they have relatively limited influence. This perspective is strongly rebutted by the Cyprus Youth Board, which points to the representation of all types of youth organisation on its Advisory Body. The Youth Board alerted the international review team to the involvement of Turkish Cypriot youth organisations on the Advisory Body and stressed the financial support it provides to youth organisations of all persuasions.

Nevertheless, it was contended repeatedly in discussions between youth organisations and the international review team that the opportunities for influence and participation by non-political and less formal youth organisations was limited 'within the system'. Those Turkish Cypriot youth organisations that were represented were just as 'political' as their Greek Cypriot counterparts; indeed, it was suggested that it was 'sister' organisations in the north of Cyprus that largely organised bi-communal activities, and there was no space for more autonomous Turkish Cypriot youth NGOs.

The international review team noted and in one way welcomed the highly politicised nature of youth organisations in Cyprus. This stood in stark contrast to other parts of Europe, where the challenge is increasingly about combating the 'democratic deficit' and working on 'civic renewal' by encouraging young people to engage in 'politics' locally and nationally. The international review team therefore commended the indisputable commitment of political youth NGOs (and especially those represented on the Administrative Board of the Cyprus Youth Board) to a range of critical youth policy issues. The team was, however, concerned about the apparent subjugation of the voice and views of a wider range of youth organisations by the dominant political paradigms.

Nowhere was this more apparent than in relation to the ubiquitous challenge of the 'Cyprus Problem' and in a forthright debate between the Cyprus Youth Board and the international review team on the subject of the 'National Youth Council'. In terms of the Cyprus Problem, there is clearly a desire among some youth organisations at least to 'break down the stereotypical messages' but this is rarely articulated in any official discourse. Indeed, though the Cyprus Youth Board, to its credit, has appointed a Turkish Cypriot associate to facilitate work between the two communities, the bi-communal work undertaken by official youth NGOs is still relatively limited. Yet the international review team gained the impression that there is considerable exchange at a less formal level between Greek Cypriot and Turkish Cypriot young people, but – because of the prevailing political situation – it cannot be acknowledged officially. Nor can those advocating such developments be involved in any formal structures or meetings. The bi-communal youth forum has, to date, had to meet beyond the shores of Cyprus, though the international review team understands that it may be permitted to meet next in Nicosia, which is a welcome development.

In its proposals to establish a Multifunctional Youth Centre in Nicosia, the Cyprus Youth Board indicates that:

"The Youth Board Administrative Offices, the office of the Pancyprian Co-ordinating Committee of Youth Centres, the Pancyprian Co-ordinating Committee of Pupils, the Supreme Student Body, and the Office of the National Youth Council will be housed at the Centre." (Budget 2004, p. 21)

As mentioned, the National Youth Council was discussed, but the international review team never met the council, which was something of a surprise, and it remained unclear exactly what it was. National Youth Councils are normally independent bodies composed of representatives of a country's national youth organisations. They are sometimes described as "representing the civil society on the youth level" (paper on National Youth Councils, p. 3). There are various documents delineating the role, purpose and structure of a 'national youth council', emanating from the European Union, the Council of Europe's Congress of Local and Regional Authorities, the United Nations General Assembly and the European Youth Forum. All speak to the need for active participation by young people in civic life, and to the national body's need for autonomy and self-determination on internal issues of structure, membership, leadership and accountability.

The 'national youth council' of Cyprus is, technically at least, the Cyprus Youth Council for International Co-operation (CyCIC), which was established in 1997 "when the need came up for Cyprus youth civil society to participate in the European Youth Forum" (paper on National Youth Councils, p. 3). The Cyprus Youth Board could not fulfil this role because of its quasi-governmental status, but it does however fund CyCIC. Like the board's Advisory Body, CyCIC has some 40 youth NGOs as members, including three Turkish Cypriot and two bi-communal NGOs. But, though CyCIC may be described in some quarters as a 'National Youth Council' and though it maintains a status as a full member of the European Youth Forum, considerable doubt was expressed to the international review team whether it fulfils the criteria to be a 'national youth council'. The main grounds for concern relate to the absence of provisions for elections to its 'Presidium', the limited level of 'state' funding available, its alleged closed membership, and its lack of social or political recognition. Indeed, the Cyprus Youth Board perceives CyCIC to be simply one member of its Advisory Body – a youth organisation focused on international links and relations.

Yet the presentation of CyCIC is very different in different documentation. For example, "the young people of Cyprus are represented at a national level by the National Youth Council, in Cyprus (CYCIC)" (Cyprus Youth Board response to EU White Paper questionnnaire on participation, p. 3). Elsewhere in the same document, it is stated that "the National Youth Council (CYCIC) operates as an advisory council to the Youth Board" (p. 7) and that "the national Youth Council of Cyprus (CYCIC), is represented at a European Level, as a member of the European Youth Forum" (p. 11). In the EU questionnaire on research, it is stated "young people, youth associations and national youth council or similar bodies were consulted in discussion prior [to] drafting this questionnaire" (Cyprus Youth Board response to EU White Paper questionnaire on greater understanding of youth, p. 17).

In contrast, when the international review team raised the matter of the 'National Youth Council' with the Cyprus Youth Board, it was told in no uncertain terms:

"It is the Cyprus Youth Council for International Co-operation. There has been some misunderstanding. It is not the national youth council. The role of a national youth council is now played by the Youth Board through its consultative committees. [CyCIC] is not a super youth organisation co-ordinating the work of all the youth NGOs in Cyprus.

It is not a question of recognition. They are heavily funded by the Youth Board ... but there were some problems. The Board wants all NGOs to work together on an equal basis in relation to the European Youth Forum. CyCIC is not above all the others. We fund them, just like we fund all the others (anti-racism, drugs, arts, etc.). We cannot tell them what to do. We have given them the opportunity to have a place on the advisory committee of the Youth Board, but that is not about co-ordinating the other NGOs."

If the CyCIC was not the 'national youth council' of Cyprus, were there plans to establish one? (The international review team was aware that the Cyprus Youth Board had put in place a number of "thematic working groups", one of which was concerned with the idea of a national youth council – and which produced the critique above.) The answer was brief: "It is not for the Board to do; it has to be the choice of the youth NGOs. This is an issue for civil society, not for the government".

There is patently considerable tension and disquiet on this issue, compounded by some negative perceptions by some youth organisations that the Cyprus Youth Board is subject to excessive political control. There are certainly some strong views expressed in this direction (though there is by no means a consensus – and others believe the board treads a very constructive line between wider politics and the professional needs of young people). It is these views that fuel demands for an independent national youth council that complies more clearly with wider international criteria:

> "It is very necessary to have and exercise more influence on behalf of young people, because Cyprus has very entrenched structures of power and there is little space for young people's autonomous decision-making. We need to have more of a voice of our own."

To this end, various youth organisations proposed, in their contribution to the draft National Report, the establishment of a National Youth Council and the parallel formation of a "Joint Youth Council on Youth Questions", which would comprise both governmental organisations (such as the Cyprus Youth Board) and non-governmental youth bodies, such as the Cyprus Youth Council (draft National Report, Culture chapter, p. 33). The international review team felt that this was a courageous proposal, which did have the potential to strengthen the civil society component of youth policy development, and perhaps provide a more credible seat at the table for youth organisations in Cyprus. It may, however, not be necessary. First, greater clarification of what exactly is the 'National Youth Council' of Cyprus is required.

Recommendation 9:

The international review team remains unclear about the identity and status of the 'National Youth Council' of Cyprus. This demands further discussion and urgent clarification.

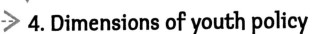

4. Dimensions of youth policy

4.1. Key domains of youth policy

4.1.1. Education, training and employment

> "Education ... ought to be the main platform for the cultivation of a new spirit of tolerance and peace for the island within an inclusive and prosperous Europe." (draft National Report, Education chapter, abstract p. 1)

During the first visit of the international review team, it was informed that a government initiative on educational reform was in progress. This reported later in the year[10] and its analysis and recommendations are wholly supported by the author of the education chapter in the draft National Report. Indeed, she remarks that "it represents the best study of the Cyprus Education system ever to be completed". The international review team had heard widespread criticism of the contemporary (Greek Cypriot) education system, maintaining that its curriculum was over-determined from the centre, that its recruitment, retention and promotion systems were outdated, that it fuelled and compounded division and hostility, and that it was out of step with the new requirements of the Cyprus economy and labour market. In short, it was out of date. All those with whom the issue was discussed agreed that there was an urgent need for change. The education chapter of the draft National Report presents a damning indictment of current educational policy and practice, highlighting a raft of deficiencies and proposing a radical overhaul of structure and administration, teacher education and training, the prescribed curriculum and teaching materials.

Since independence in 1960, education has always contributed to the divisions on the island. The constitution decreed there should be two education councils for the two communities. Since 1974 the Republic of Cyprus Government has had a Ministry of Education, one of the maximum of ten ministries permitted by the constitution. Notwithstanding the differences between Greek Cypriot and Turkish Cypriot education, there is enormous commitment to, participation in and achievement in formal education. However, this has produced a problem of overqualification and emigration in both communities, though Greek Cypriot young people are more likely than Turkish Cypriot young people to return after studying abroad – even if they can only find employment at a level below their qualifications.

---

10. Educational Reform Committee (2004), *Democratic and Humanistic Education and Culture in the Eurocyprian State*, Nicosia, August 2004.

The difficulty for the international review team was to get any sense of how education was provided (and received) beyond the framework of the Greek Cypriot community. The team did visit two schools – a 'traditional' primary school in the mountains near Paphos and a pioneering and progressive ZEP (Zone of Educational Priority) school in Limassol. In the former school, the team met the local education inspector as well as the head teacher, and enjoyed the calm and well-ordered atmosphere of the learning environment. Few difficulties or challenges were identified by those spoken to. The fixed curriculum was delivered, largely without difficulty, and in the afternoons the children were occupied with coaching classes, computers and English-language lessons. The inspector described his role in terms of assessment, administration and advice. He outlined new teaching methodologies around co-operative learning, group work and active learning. When asked about the highly prescribed curriculum, he acknowledged that a recurrent complaint from teachers was that it was "overcrowded", but said that its content was a matter of political decision "and teachers don't have much right to comment".

None of the children at the school visited was not Greek Orthodox, though the international review team was told that some 4.5% of pupils in primary education generally are from immigrant backgrounds – from countries such as Syria, Lebanon, Egypt, Russia and Turkey. There were also "gypsies" from the Turkish Cypriot area (the north) and, because there was no educational culture in their families, there was a high absenteeism rate: "it is difficult to keep them in school, but we are trying". Psychologists and welfare officers are employed to support such children. It was acknowledged that the national curriculum has not yet been sufficiently adapted to take account of new (more multicultural) circumstances, and it was agreed that, because of the strong educational traditions "here", there would be a lot of resistance to change. That was "natural", but change was certainly necessary. The international review team was told that "revisions" were being considered, and that there was now a greater level of co-operation between the Turkish Cypriot Association of Teachers and the Greek Cypriot Association of Teachers. Teachers, it was argued, always have "a key role to play in developing tolerance in children".

The international review team gradually established a view that there were three essential concerns about the formal education system in Cyprus:

- Issues concerning tolerance and intercultural learning and understanding
- Space for attention to personal, health and social issues
- The relationship with the labour market

The Common Declaration of the Bi-Communal Youth Forum states that institutions, such as those in the field of education, must take on the role of "promoting rapprochement, co-operation and friendship between both communities" and

"must refrain from creating and eternising negative stereotypes towards one another, whilst respecting aspects of pluralism. In this perception, history books should be reviewed to reflect all the realities, both negative and positive. Also, for the development of a culture of peaceful co-existence, it is of vital importance that the youth are introduced to the language used by the other community as a second language. All of these will contribute to the development of mutual understanding and respect." (Bi-communal Youth Forum, Common Declaration, Budapest, 30 March 2002, pp. 1-2)

As one student noted to the international review team, young people are often more open-minded and the oldest people can recall the days of co-existence. It is the middle generation – who currently have political and professional influence and authority – who do of course know of the days of displacement, disappearances, conflict and entrenchment, and for these reasons understandably find it most difficult to embrace new thinking and perspectives on change and development. And education is the site where such new approaches will be pivotal.

The international review team's visit to the ZEP school in Limassol saw a model of good practice in action and a prospective catalyst for reform. The school, in a poor area occupied by Turkish Cypriots before the 1974 invasion, faces challenges not only of multiculturalism but also of low cultural commitment to education. Students experience many difficulties at home (including violence) and in the community (for example, drugs), which clearly affect their capacity to learn. Both within the school and at the interface between school and community, there are initiatives to address the wider learning and development needs of young people. Moreover, the school has established constructive links with other schools in the area, with parents and with local business. There is another ZEP school in Nicosia; the international review team was told that there is not only cross-fertilisation of experience and ideas between the ZEP schools but also communication with the Ministry of Education, which is watching their progress with considerable interest.

Recommendation 10:

Though the international review team has not had sight of the Education Reform Committee's report, it feels that the arguments made both in the education chapter of the National Report and the practice model of the ZEP schools present a way forward for the much-needed reform of the (Greek) Cypriot education system. This is critical for intercultural learning and mutual understanding, though it is also likely to meet wider learning and development objectives.

A recurrent complaint expressed to the international review team was that the educational curriculum in Cyprus is so 'packed' with academic learning that it leaves little space for attention to wider personal and developmental issues. Indeed, beyond formal schooling, the preoccupation among Cypriots with academic achievement meant that leisure time was often dedicated to additional coaching and language classes. Yet in the extensive documentation on current programmes on youth-related issues, the Ministry of Education and Culture appears to have taken a strong lead on health, environmental and heritage issues. Such educative and preventative programmes are to be welcomed, though the international review team remains uninformed about their prevalence or their content. A challenge for any modern learning curriculum is the balance struck between such 'personal, social and health' education initiatives and more traditional academic study.

Young Cypriots, from both the south and north of the island, are extremely well-educated. The problem they face is that of overqualification and underemployment. Ironically, there is far less unemployment among young people who do not pursue tertiary education and opt instead for more technical routes into the labour market, however much this may be perceived as a 'second-rate' option. Those who do sustain their academic education tend to aspire to employment in the public sector, which is more rewarding and more secure than the private sector.

Unemployment in Cyprus remains very low (at a little over 3%), though young people are disproportionately represented within the unemployed population (but this is still the third lowest youth unemployment rate within the European Union). The highest level of youth unemployment is among higher education graduates, though this is largely explained by their struggle to gain jobs that correspond to their qualifications and their willingness to wait (usually supported by their families) until they have exhausted such possibilities – and many, ultimately, settle for less.

In the north of Cyprus, the literacy rate is about 99% and there are six universities. There is a similar commitment to, and engagement in, education among Turkish Cypriots, though less among young people from the settler population. The international review team was told that continued participation in education was a means (for young men) of postponing military service and that the quality of higher education was questionable: it was more of a business proposition and the second largest 'economy' in the north. As in the south, the aspiration of most young people was to work for the 'government'. Also as in the south, there was a sense of insecurity about the labour market and a high prevalence of underemployment: "if you work for the government, you know you have a reasonable level of security and will get the 'salary you signed for' at the end of the month". Many Cypriots in the north also go to study or work abroad but, unlike their counterparts in the south, many do not return. The Turkish Cypriots consulted on these matters estimated that more than three-quarters of their contemporaries were very likely to emigrate.

Recommendation 11:

The international review team felt that more attention needed to be given to the small, but steadily increasing, population of young people who are not Greek or Turkish Cypriots, in order to have more reliable data on their education and employment circumstances, and thereby to address any emergent issues.

The international review team was struck by the parallel accounts of circumstances in both education and employment of young Greek and Turkish Cypriots. Both 'stories' were told with conviction and certainty. What was not mentioned, however, and what led the international review team to feel that it had acquired only a partial picture of the situation, was any account of the circumstances of 'other' young people in Cyprus and 'other' labour markets. When the team was informed that "nobody who is Greek Cypriot educated is going to work as a worker", this inevitably begged the question of who did fulfil the more menial functions in Cypriot society: building roads and servicing the tourist industry. There were no more than glimpses of answers to this question. For example, though only a handful of Turkish Cypriots study at the University of Cyprus, some 13 000 cross the Green Line each day for work. A Farmers' Union representative informed the international review team that there were some 4 000 Turkish Cypriots employed in the south, within the wider observation that "co-existence is possible, despite the problems". A representative of another trade union commented that "foreign workers were on the increase", producing unfair competition due to illegal employment and general problems of decreasing wages, improper working conditions and insufficient health and safety provision. It was estimated that some 13% of the workforce comprised legitimate foreign workers, but it was suggested that there might be a similar number working illegally.

Youth policy in Cyprus

Beyond the high level of public sector employment (a 'youth policy' strategy in itself), the government has instituted a range of special initiatives, such as provision to encourage new farmers (to combat emigration from the land) and computer training for those undergoing military service. Two more general measures in the field of training and employment have been vocational apprenticeship training programmes for early leavers from education (under the Ministry of Labour), and an increasing commitment to 'enterprise' training and support (under the Ministry of Commerce, Industry and Tourism). Both seem to be essential measures, the first to alleviate demand for skilled artisans, the second to reduce the pressure on the public sector and its unsustainable fiscal deficit and public debt. Further new training programmes have recently been introduced by the Human Resource Development Agency, concerned with training and employability, vocational counselling and guidance, and women not currently in the labour force. There is also an intention to establish a new level of education, between secondary and higher education. This is to be called Continuous Technical-Professional Education (CTPE) and will commence in 2005-6 (draft National Report, Employment chapter, p. 15).

Cyprus has recently established a National Committee for Employment, whose responsibility is to oversee implementation of a national employment strategy. Analysis by the University of Cyprus suggests that six key issues require attention in relation to young people:

- The enhancement of career counselling services
- The professionalisation of small (usually family) businesses
- Greater parity of esteem for technical education
- Research to establish the relationships between education and employment
- Improved public information to enable young people to make more informed choices about future education and labour market trajectories
- Efforts to correct the distortion arising from the gulf in salaries and working conditions between the public and private sector (draft National Report, Employment chapter, pp. 16-18)

These points are discussed in detail in the employment chapter of the draft National Report. The ideas make sense to the international review team, which believes that they would repay serious consideration. In the wider Europe, there is a wealth of practice on these fronts, distributed across different countries, from which Cyprus could usefully draw.

Recommendation 12:

The international review team welcomed the critical analysis of the current relationships between education and the labour market, produced by the University of Cyprus, and felt that its proposals were consistent with training and labour market initiatives which have been seen as a necessary component of 'youth policy' in other parts of Europe.

4.1.2. Youth work and non-formal education

Non-formal learning (otherwise known as 'youth work' or associative life) is one of the main strands of work within the Youth Directorate of the Council of Europe, which has pioneered a range of pedagogical methodologies over many years, through its commitment to human rights education and intercultural learning. Most recently it has, in partnership with the European Commission, established a Europe-wide training programme (the ATTE course),[11] the first cohort of which completed the two-year course in October 2003. It has also engaged in the pan-European debate on the increasing role of non-formal learning within the 'learning pathways' of young people, and the question of its recognition, accreditation and validation.[12]

Within the framework of the EU's ten-year 'Lisbon strategy' on lifelong learning, there is now the Copenhagen/Brugge convention on vocational training, within which a robust discussion is taking place on life-wide learning – learning that can take place 'beyond the classroom' and beyond formal structures of education – in other words, through non-formal mechanisms that support personal development and the acquisition of 'soft skills' such as problem-solving, decision-making and communication. Non-formal learning is person-centred and significantly experiential, drawing from and building on the motivation and competences of participants, guided by facilitators and trainers rather than 'teachers'.

There appeared in Cyprus to be a rather limited theoretical understanding of the idea of 'youth work' and an empirical lack of space for its provision or development. There was a strange entry in one document: "The Youth Centre Institution has been present since 1968 and operates at too fast a pace" (Governing Board of the Cyprus Youth Board, Strategic Plan for the Directions of the 1999-2003 Five-Year Period, p. 3). The international review team felt that, given this lengthy history of youth-centre provision, there might have been a more persuasive articulation of their place and purpose. The Cyprus Youth Board told the team that it was currently dealing with 'non-formal education', but it remained unclear what that meant. Indeed, beyond the occasional reference to the concept in official discourse, and some discussion of it at the Youth Information Centre and with some youth NGOs, the topic was conspicuous only by its absence. When the subject was raised by the international review team, it was frequently conflated with coaching courses and individual activity choices during leisure time after compulsory schooling. One respondent informed the team that:

> "Non-formal learning in Cyprus is private education, things like music and sports. There are coaching classes every afternoon, so there is a different distribution of 'free time' and 'leisure' compared to other places in Europe."

There is, of course, the network of about a hundred 'youth clubs' in the rural areas of Cyprus and the proposed development of 'multifunctional youth centres'. The international review team commended such development, but was concerned to hear that "youth centres are really just a gathering place for young people; they don't have a lot of work going on". There is nothing wrong with the provision of 'gathering places' but, for non-formal education to take place, things have to go further than that. The young people in Kato Pyrgos told the international review team that they wanted activities and leadership, and this raises questions about the programme and the staffing within such provision. In essence, non-formal learning contexts require three things:

11. Advanced Training for Trainers in Europe, developed through a Quality and Curriculum Working Group established under a training covenant between the Council of Europe and the European Commission.

12. At the time of writing, January 2005, a seminar is planned in Belgium on "Bridges for Recognition", a follow-up to the "Bridges to Training" seminar held in Belgium in September 2001.

- Places to meet
- Projects to undertake
- People to provide appropriate support

The international review team struggled to understand exactly what goes on within the current 'non-formal' youth provision in Cyprus: what kinds of issues are addressed or programmes undertaken; what kinds of staff make this happen and to what kind of training (if any) they have access. The team did hear about some of the difficulties of securing buildings and some issues concerning the possibility of a local political 'veto' on the content of programmes (activities or issues). The fundamental point about non-formal learning is that it provides some level of autonomous space: a context and opportunity for self-organisation by young people on issues of concern to them. There are now, of course, possibilities to engage in virtual communities, through the use of new technologies, which hold the promise of connecting the local to the global. The issues that are routinely addressed in 'youth work' practice are legion: sexuality, health, internationalism and multiculturalism, as well as debates around vocational pathways or opportunities for trips away from home.

Many of these issues are already addressed in 'youth policy' in Cyprus – within schools, at the Youth Information Centres or through school camping trips. The point being made by the international review team is that while the content may now be on the agenda, there is a case for reflecting on the suitability of the context and method through which such issues are currently being tackled. Non-formal learning may be a substitute for existing approaches or an important supplement to them. The international review team was acutely aware that there appears to be little tradition of person-centred, collective practice in Cyprus and that, given that prevailing culture, it may be 'too much, too soon' to consider some of the approaches suggested. Nevertheless, given the attention currently afforded to non-formal learning elsewhere in Europe, there is a strong case for debating how, in Cyprus, a framework might be developed to strengthen its contribution to the learning opportunities for young people.

> **Recommendation 13:**
>
> The international review team welcomes the infrastructure already in place for the development of non-formal learning opportunities for young people. It believes, however, that there needs to be a deeper exploration of the nature of provision and of the 'professional' skills applied by those who work with young people in this context.

4.1.3. Health

Notwithstanding the extensive population survey on drug abuse (misuse) undertaken by the Open Therapeutic Community of Addicted,[13] the international review team found itself being pulled all over the place on health questions affecting young people. Illegal drugs were the dominant focus of attention and discussion, and indeed they take up a quarter of the president's Governance Programme on Youth Policy. They are also prominent in the document 'Current programmes on

---

13. Boyiadjis, G. (2003), *Steps for Prevention of Drug Abuse: findings of Pancyprian general population survey – 2003*, Open Therapeutic Community of Addicted.

Dimensions of youth policy

youth-related issues', and in the work of the Ministry of Health and the Ministry of Education. The Cyprus Youth Board has its own dedicated anti-drugs helpline, and a 'reformed' anti-drugs council will now be responsible for taking forward a strategy for combating substance misuse in Cyprus.

There is a general consensus that there has been a dramatic increase in drug misuse by young people and a corresponding 'explosion' in drug-related crime. This has been attributed to four key factors: the Turkish invasion and subsequent social problems arising from geographical and social dislocation; rapid urbanisation; contact with the drugs culture by Cypriots studying abroad; and the rise in tourism (draft National Report, Crime chapter, pp. 8-9). The 'opening' of Cyprus in a variety of ways has clearly produced the kinds of social 'dislocation' that are unequivocally the cause of various psycho-social problems, including drug misuse (Rutter and Smith 1995).

Understanding the prevalence, nature and impact of drug misuse is, for all countries, a major challenge. The 'drugs culture' is clearly of major concern, to the individuals affected by it and the communities around them. Nevertheless, the focus on illegal drugs (whether in relation to preventative education, health treatment services or law enforcement) can sometimes have the effect of diverting attention away from more prevalent, and ultimately more dangerous, health issues affecting young people: notably diet, obesity, smoking and alcohol use and, not just in the case of Cyprus, traffic accidents. There is also increasing concern about sexually transmitted infections and the risks of HIV/AIDS.

As the international review team put it, there is therefore a 'panorama' of issues to be addressed. It is too big a question to be addressed in detail and anyway Cyprus already appears to have a range of de facto and proposed strategies and structures in place (for example, the Ministry of Health's HIV/AIDS Strategic Plan 2004-8, the Anti-Drugs Council, and the proposals within the 'Cyprus youth policy formulation' on sexual and reproductive health, teenage pregnancy and HIV/AIDS). There is also the health chapter of the draft National Report prepared by the University of Cyprus. This addresses demographic issues, health services, obesity and eating disorders, drug abuse, smoking and alcohol, teenage pregnancy, HIV/AIDS and road-traffic accidents. The international review team will therefore restrict its remarks to a few points that it considers of particular pertinence.

The health levels of young Cypriots are generally very good, but this should not conceal areas of considerable concern. The traditional healthy Cypriot diet is being increasingly replaced by the consumption of less healthy food. There have also been significant increases in eating disorders such as anorexia and bulimia, especially among young women. These issues of diet, exercise, obesity and eating disorders have been thoroughly researched in three recent studies (see draft National Report, Health chapter, pp. 4-6). Young people in Cyprus tend to be poly-drug users, but the statistics do not differentiate between 'triers', 'users' and 'problem users', categories which are now considered to be a critical basis for policy analysis and development, beneath the 'headline' figures for increasing usage and lifetime data. In Cyprus, it is not clear whether there should be greater concern or some sense of reassurance about the research evidence that some 97% of young people believe they know how to protect themselves against drugs. This could be a laudable outcome of preventative education or it could be worrying evidence of self-delusion among Cypriot youth. Certainly illegal drugs are widely available: 83% of young people said that it was easy for someone to obtain drugs (ibid., p. 8).

Cyprus holds "one of the top places in the world in terms of tobacco consumption" and the incidence of smoking is higher among younger age groups; alcohol use is similar, "embedded in the Greek Cypriot culture", with the most frequent drinkers also being in the younger age groups. In the draft National Report, the availability and accessibility of cigarettes is described as a key factor in explaining youth smoking behaviour; from wider research evidence, the same is true of alcohol consumption. Price and availability are the most significant determinants of usage (Edwards et al. 1994).

Cyprus has one of the lowest proportions of extra-marital births in Europe, though there is an increasing trend in unwanted pregnancies and abortion. The draft National Report notes, however, that there are limited data on the current situation in relation to teenage pregnancy and calls for more systematic empirical research. The rate of HIV infection is also very low (0.1%), with only 16 new infections in 2002 (involving 7 Cypriots and 16 foreigners).

Road-traffic accidents can be a major cause of injury and death among young people (along with cancer and suicide), but they appear to be an especially serious problem in Cyprus. About one third of those killed in traffic accidents in 2003 and 2004 were young people under 25. The primary causes of the accidents, according to the police, were speeding, careless driving and alcohol consumption (draft National Report, Health chapter, p. 14). Various 'traffic-awareness' education programmes have, accordingly, been introduced in schools, as well as stricter penalties for traffic violations.

The draft National Report outlines a range of recommendations, most of which are fully supported by the international review team, except for the one advocating 'fear' campaigns in the mass media – depicting in graphic detail the stark consequences of teenage pregnancies, drug use, smoking or road accidents. The basis of this recommendation is its alleged effectiveness in "attracting attention, maintaining interest, stimulating thinking and persuading people to behave in a desirable manner" (draft National Report, Health chapter, p. 15). Those are of course what any educational or preventative programme seeks to achieve, but the international review team is not aware (though the author of the health chapter of the draft National Report may know) of robust research evidence that the 'fear' factor is of use in this.

The international review team was generally impressed with the analysis and attention to health issues affecting young people. It was, however, concerned about the question of balance – in the weight attached to different health issues (especially the almost obsessive attention to illegal drug misuse), in the relationship between strategy and delivery, and in the apparent preference for 'high-threshold' programmes at the expense of lower-level interventions. This is a crude representation of such concerns, for the team was aware that some balance has clearly been struck. The international review team believes, nevertheless, that the balance needs to be struck even more firmly in the direction of (a) broader health issues affecting young people, (b) greater attention to the quality and context of delivery, and (c) more grounded, community-based education, counselling and treatment interventions.

Secondly, the international review team was concerned at the lack of data relating to the health of young Turkish Cypriots in the north. Once more, it recognises the difficulties of accessing such information and the team had to depend upon a qualitative insight. It was told that an experts' group from Brussels had concluded that there were few prominent health issues in the north. There were, for example, few STIs, low rates of teenage suicide (though it was greatest in the army), relatively few teenage pregnancies, and not (yet) an emergence of eating disorders or obesity ("We don't have MacDonalds"!). On the other hand, there were significant levels of smoking and drinking among young people, and a huge prevalence of cancer later in life. There is no special health education or sexual health provision for teenagers, but there is one treatment centre for those presenting problematic drug misuse. Drugs are cheap to buy and very accessible, contributing to high levels of drug-related crime.

The international review team recognises that currently there is not much that can be done by the Republic of Cyprus Government to address these issues. Nevertheless, it would still be useful to collect and collate any available data on the health circumstances of young people in the north of the island, if only – at the moment – to reflect upon commonalities and differences. In time, it may be necessary to establish a differentiated, calibrated health policy for young people in different parts of the island, in response to their different needs.

Finally, the international review team felt there was insufficient attention to promoting positive health as against preventing negative health. Health issues appeared compartmentalised rather than inter-connected, despite the rhetoric on overall lifestyles and the need to build 'self-esteem'. There were many illustrations of excellent analysis and practice (those of the Open Therapeutic Communities, the Cyprus Family Planning Association and KENTHEA, an umbrella group for anti-drugs practice, come to mind), but they did not appear to fit within an overarching strategy. In the field of drug misuse, the anti-drugs council is in the process of building a strategy and infrastructure, but that by definition is restricted to the issue of drugs.

The international review team was told that the government 'is for pluralism, so that people have a choice'. This position is to be respected, but it should be choices within an overall vision and framework, one that accommodates the range of health challenges facing young people across departmental responsibilities and at different levels of provision and practice. Such a vision needs to set out a philosophical position based not simply on the 'eradication' of health problems but also possibly on 'harm reduction', and of course on education and prevention.

Recommendation 14:

The international review team encountered much progressive thinking about the health of young people in Cyprus and corresponding measures to address it. This work on policy and practice was, however, constrained by the absence of any overarching thinking about the weight (and therefore resources) to be attached to different issues, the most desired philosophies and methodologies, and connections between different health challenges, and also an imbalance in the data available. The production of a cross-departmental framework plan aimed at supporting the positive health of young people in Cyprus as well as combating health-risk behaviour would seem to be desirable. This might be entitled 'The Health of the Young Nation'.

4.1.4. Housing

The vast majority of young people in Cyprus remain living in their parental home until they get married. There is a range of housing policy initiatives in Cyprus, administered through the Ministry of Interior. These are focused on particular groups (such as low-income families) or on particular issues (such as sustaining the population of small communities or encouraging residence in the buffer zone). The international review team was told that there is no special public provision or consideration of housing for young people. When young people are ready to leave home, they tend to receive considerable family support and anyway benefit from a bouyant labour market. If not, they live 'at home'.

The international review team raised the issue of 'youth homelessness' on a number of occasions, but this appeared to be an alien concept. Only during a visit to a children's home was the prospect of young people becoming homeless considered as an issue. The children's home did not provide for young people beyond the age of 18, but it was argued that young men over that age would then enter military service (and still be assisted by the state), while young women were likely to proceed further in their education (and therefore be supported by the Ministry of Finance). It was conceded that some children ("difficult teenagers") did run away; this was considered a matter for the police, psychologists and the social welfare department.

There may, currently, be little need to consider the issue of housing for young people. However, two factors may change this situation in the relatively near future. The rate of family breakdown has increased significantly in recent years (the numbers of divorces trebled between 1992 and 2001) and the 'immigrant' population of Cyprus is also on the increase. Immigrants may not have the same cultural traditions or physical opportunity for the kind of 'family protection' that has historically prevailed in Cyprus. Elsewhere in Europe, housing has become more prominent as a component of public youth policy, as affordable accommodation in the private market becomes more elusive and as more and more single and unsupported young people seek independent living. This may be a matter for future consideration in the youth policy of Cyprus.

4.1.5. Social protection

The international review team heard occasional references to the "social welfare department" but gained no real sense of the extent to which it offered financial or other protection to young people 'in need'. As with housing, it is assumed that the strength of Cypriot (extended) family tradition continues to provide the requisite support for the vast majority of young people.

Yet all was not completely rosy in the garden! The international review team's visit to the Women's Information and Support Centre (Apanemi) in Limassol indicated clearly that the prevalence of risk and domestic violence to women and their children is on the increase (or, perhaps more accurately, is increasingly coming to public attention, with women no longer tolerating such circumstances). In its short existence, Apanemi has provided services to some 350 women. The staff at Apanemi confirmed that official statistics (based on reports to the police) were little more than the tip of an iceberg. Moreover, there were now women from other countries who, after short relationships, were being abandoned or ejected by their Cypriot partners.[14] Most of those who have used Apanemi's services to date are young women (up to the age of 30). Apanemi also highlighted the increasing challenge of responding to the needs of vulnerable women who were immigrants, refugees or asylum seekers in Cyprus.

14. The Human Rights Commissioner noted that "likewise, several foreign women are liable to expulsion because of relationships which they have attempted to form with a Cypriot man or because they have broken off such a relationship" (Council of Europe, Report by Mr Alvaro Gil-Robles, the Commissioner for Human Rights, on his visit to Cyprus 25-29 June 2003, p. 6).

Dimensions of youth policy

Suffice it to say here that there is likely to be an enlarging gap between what the family provides for its members (including its young people) and what the state provides. This 'gap' may currently be relatively small, but it will certainly increase. The question around 'social protection' is twofold: To what extent should state resources be directed to plugging the gap? And should the state be directly responsible for plugging the gap or should it support the development of an NGO infrastructure to do so? Apanemi would appear to be a good model for the latter – an organisation providing public 'goods' through civil society.

4.1.6. Family policy and child welfare

The international review team was told constantly and repeatedly of the sustaining strength of the Cypriot family structure within local communities as the bedrock for the nurture and support of children and young people. "People stay local", it was informed, "the family is paramount". Clearly this does not apply to all children and young people. The social welfare services, under the Ministry of Labour and Social Insurance, make residential and community provision for children with severe learning difficulties, and for those presenting delinquent and behavioural problems (see below). It also provides daycare services for school-age children, aged 6-18, after school hours, while their parents are at work ("Current programmes on youth-related issues", pp. 13-16).

The international review team visited a children's home in Limassol for sixteen children aged 6-12 who had been neglected by their parents and become wards of the state. Other children are in foster care or remain in the parental home, but under the supervision of the social welfare services. The international review team was told there are some 90 children in foster care in the Limassol area and 'thousands' under supervision in the country as a whole. In the children's home, those resident were from a range of backgrounds: Turkish and Greek Cypriots, mixed backgrounds, British Cypriots and one of unknown parentage.

It was impossible for the international review team to discern an accurate sense of 'need' for child welfare and perhaps 'for family policy' in Cyprus. Once more, however, there was some concern that such 'need' remained rather camouflaged, with a focus on Greek Cypriot culture and traditions (which themselves are not everything they are sometimes proclaimed to be), at the expense of attention to the probable different circumstances of other groups. Only at the ZEP school in Limassol did the international review team encounter an appropriate level of analysis, understanding and intervention in relation to parents from various backgrounds, in order to provide appropriate support for the young people concerned.

> **Recommendation 15:**
>
> In the Council of Europe guidelines on youth policy development (Council of Europe 2003b), there is a discussion of both a 'knowledge gap' and an 'implementation gap'. The former is the vacuum between research and policy, the second the vacuum between policy and practice. The international review team felt that there was a 'knowledge gap' in relation to (especially) non-Greek Cypriots and their housing, social protection and social welfare. This needs to be rectified before any 'implementation gap' can be considered.

4.1.7. Leisure and culture

Young people's leisure time appears to be consumed significantly by education (within and beyond the school) and home-based family life. At the junior school, the international review team was told that children spent too much time playing on computers; that is, when they were not engaged in coaching courses and other extra-curricular activity. The young people of secondary school age in Kato Pyrgos bemoaned the fact they had no recreational facilities and said they spent their time watching television or playing sports. Most had travelled abroad, for holidays. They said they did a range of things in the school holidays:[15] studying, swimming, fishing, reading, sports, hunting, work, computers, cycling and walking. All of them had a computer at home and used it both for playing games and for study.

These accounts suggest a context of well-structured, constructive learning and leisure. The international review team wondered, however, about the encroachment of tourism on this way of life and its impact on the behaviour, culture and beliefs of young Cypriots. It was curious to know of the relation between these 'healthy' lifestyles and the anxieties expressed elsewhere about the all-pervasive drugs culture. It reflected on the effects of globalisation and Europeanisation.

Government policy on leisure and culture appears to focus on what might be called 'high culture': theatre and dance, festivals and the cultural heritage of the island. The Cyprus Youth Board has indeed been commended for supporting alternative, more 'bottom-up' approaches, through initiatives that bring different groups of young people together to engage in mutual learning, rather than continuing to engage in a 'nationalistic discourse'. The international review team sees 'culture' as a key mechanism for the production of 'identity'; and clearly, among Greek Cypriots, a selective use of 'culture' has promoted a particular version of Greek Cypriot 'identity'. There was a view from the international review team that there were now opportunities to use new forms of 'culture' to allow for a new form of European Cypriot identity. After all, new cultural industries were emerging, and new hybrid forms of music and film were available (most Greek Cypriots of a certain age grew up with just one television channel).

And there would no doubt be an increasing cultural influence by immigrant minority youth, if patterns elsewhere were to be replicated, even if currently "everybody knows they are here, but nobody knows who they are". Closer to home, it was noted on more than one occasion that Turkish Cypriots from the north would soon be studying at the University of Cyprus (a few already are), bringing to bear an alternative, indigenous, cultural perspective.

As in all communities, there are inevitably competing cultural forces and in Cyprus, for young men, there is, of course, the culture of the army. Conscription serves to reinforce a particular (Greek) Cypriot identity, positioned against the 'other' (notably the Turkish invader) – and some very different respondents spoke critically of the impact of military service on young men in the formative years. Not that they objected per se to military service, and they usually saw the need for it in the current circumstances, but they suggested that there should be greater flexibility in the age at which young men were required to fulfil their military obligations.

The culture chapter in the draft National Report engages powerfully with the prevailing cultural context of Cyprus, pulling few punches but equally seeking to address questions across a wide spectrum of issues. An especially pertinent observation for those deluded into any romantic perspective about 'bridge-building' across the community divide was that:

"A dominant concern about bi-communal youth activities, until recently, was that the workshops compromised historical truth for the sake of building a cul-

15. All were Greek Cypriots, though a couple had been adopted from abroad, but were described as "well accepted in the community". Their holiday destinations had been diverse: Greece, England, Spain, Portugal, France, Finland, Egypt and Syria.

ture of peace and substituted a superficial community building for the depth of memory." (draft National Report, Culture chapter, p. 13)

Less mythology and more acceptance of (often tragic) human experiences on both sides, rather than expedient political constructions, were critical steps towards healing processes, in which shared cultural experiences were an additional building block. So, although still focused on many shared Cypriot traditions (both Greek and Turkish), the Cyprus Family Planning Association has argued for learning about the 'other':

> "Meeting with other cultures and learning of alternatives to their own reality, and also cultivating their thought and directing it towards analysing the choices they make, would lead Cypriot youth toward a change of mentalities that disallow the free expression of their thought and body and thus their completion as free individuals." (Cyprus Youth Policy formulation, Suggestions on youth policy for 'Youth and Culture', from Youth for Youth, Cyprus Family Planning Association, p. 4)

On the same theme, a Turkish Cypriot NGO also made proposals around dance, handicrafts, cuisine and costumes, but was explicit in emphasising that the objectives of any cultural policy

> "are to promote a common cultural area characterised by its cultural diversity and shared cultural heritage in Cyprus. It seeks to encourage cultural creation and mobility, access to culture for all, the dissemination of art and culture, intercultural dialogue and knowledge and history of the Cypriots. These objectives will also accord culture a social integration and socio-economic development role." (Proposal for the development of a National Youth Policy of Cyprus from the TKP Youth Branch, on Youth and 'Culture', p. 2)

There appear to be enormous opportunities to, almost literally, cultivate the old and the new, the high and the 'low', the deeply-rooted and newly-planted elements of culture in Cyprus. The country's new status as a member of the European Union opens up a cultural playground for young people who, if they are not yet ready to explore their rich cultural heritage across their two indigenous communities, can exploit the possibilities for intercultural dialogue and understanding through contact with, and exploration of, new immigrant culture and the culture of communities elsewhere. Through doing so, they are likely to become more willing and more receptive to similar engagement in their own 'back yard', a process which has started in some quarters, but which is understandably difficult.

Recommendation 16:

The international review team believes that strengthened contact and engagement with diversity and difference across cultures, which is already starting through immigration and tourism as well as participation in the wider Europe, is an important catalyst for intercultural tolerance and understanding. It should, where possible, be supported and encouraged by the Cyprus Youth Board and other parts of the Republic of Cyprus Government.

4.1.8. Youth justice

The crime chapter of the draft National Report provides a strong critique of the ways in which the criminal justice system in Cyprus deals with its young offenders (delinquents). Based strongly on an old-fashioned, and now largely discredited, British system, there is some movement towards more 'modern' provision, control and intervention, but as yet there appears to be little consideration of measures such as more calibrated and individualised community penalties or the application of restorative justice.

There was widespread consensus that youth crime in Cyprus (and not just drug-related acquisitive crime) is on the increase, with staggering percentage increases for some, especially more serious offences (for details, see draft National Report, Crime chapter, p. 5). Dramatic increases in offending have taken place in both the south and the north of the island (though they appear to have been rather less dramatic in the north). By international comparisons, however, Cyprus still enjoys relatively low crime rates; as elsewhere, it is "excessive media coverage of some offences [that] has been largely responsible for the public's fear of crime" (ibid., p. 3). Nevertheless, youth offending is a cause for concern; the major challenge is to establish a response that will prevent the occurrence of further offending. The system for dealing with young offenders, however, is described as:

> "anachronistic and wanting in a number of significant ways, including legislative provisions, the training of judges, the complete absence of other court personnel, the absence of a probation service and any institutions for juveniles, whether open communities or secure." (ibid., p. 4)

Juvenile cases (those between 10, the age of criminal responsibility, and 16) are within the remit of untrained social workers and, though provision for community service orders was made as long ago as 1996, they still cannot be used because the necessary personnel have yet to be appointed. Those under 14 who commit minor offences are referred by the police to the Department of Social Welfare, where they are treated as children in need of care and protection, rather than as young offenders. Those who appear before the court do so in what is theoretically a 'juvenile court' but is in fact an adult court, being used on days or at times set aside for juvenile hearings. "A proper juvenile court is long overdue", according to the draft National Report, a view reiterated by the President of the House Standing Committee on Criminal Affairs, Mr Costas Papacostas. In his address to the international review team, he articulated the concerns and commendable analysis of his committee:

> "The social problem of juvenile delinquency has its roots within the institutions that compose a society, such as *family*, *education* and the *mass media*. The solution to this problem, therefore, must be searched with such institutions." (Mr Costas Papacostas, Member of the Cyprus Parliament, President of the House Standing Committee on Criminal Affairs, welcome speech to the international review team, p. 1; emphasis original)

Mr Papacostas went on to outline proposals to assist parents and families, social intervention initiatives, greater support in schools, an improved infrastructure for constructive leisure (multifunctional youth centres and camping areas) and regulation of the media. Significantly, he also stated the 'absolute necessity' of establishing a Juvenile Court for Minors, and he announced the establishment of a Board for the Prevention of Crime.[16]

---

16. In the UK since 1998, under the auspices of the quasi-independent Youth Justice Board, the primary objective of the youth justice system has been the prevention of offending or further offending. Official responses to young offenders are based around the three 'R's of responsibility, restoration and re-integration, in recognition of the fact that, while proportionality should remain a feature of sentencing, 'making good' and being re-presented with mainstream opportunities are also necessary if there is to be victim satisfaction and some prospect of offenders re-orientating the course of their lives in a more purposeful and law-abiding direction.

"This would be established mainly for the definition of a common policy, with regards to the prevention of Crime, the support of research on crime and the co-ordination of prevention services." (Mr Costas Papacostas, Member of the Cyprus Parliament, President of the House Standing Committee on Criminal Affairs, welcome speech to the international review team, p. 2)

The international review team welcomes these proposals. Old philosophies around addressing 'juvenile delinquency' (both 'treatment' and 'punishment' models) are now largely discredited, having served neither societies nor individual young people well. New, more creative, approaches have been developed in many parts of the world (notably in New Zealand, but also England and Wales), from which Cyprus might draw some useful ideas for adaptation and application in its own specific context.

Recommendation 17:

The international review team was concerned to read, in the draft National Report, the somewhat damning critique of the current youth justice system in Cyprus. It welcomes the initiatives being taken through the Parliamentary Committee on Criminal Affairs in relation to more constructive approaches to dealing with young offenders and believes that such a trajectory should be pursued.

4.1.9. National defence and military service

This is sometimes considered a contentious element of 'youth policy', but it is a reality for young people in some countries and may serve individual needs as well as societal ones. This was certainly apparent in Finland, where the first Council of Europe international review of national youth policy took place, in 1997 (Williamson 1999). In Cyprus, military service is clearly a big issue for young people on both sides of the divide. Unfortunately, the international review team had no opportunity to speak to serving soldiers, apart from one sentry whose sole remark was that he "would rather not be here". Young people from Turkish Cypriot NGOs told the team that, in the north, high participation rates in higher education were partly explained as a strategy for 'wriggling out' of or at least deferring having to serve in the military.

In other countries, military service can serve as a rite of passage whereby young people (men, in most cases) leave home and acquire personal and practical skills. In Cyprus, however, young men who are conscripted generally do not leave home, living in barracks while on duty and returning home when they are not. The international review team was told that most of their duties were "mind-numbingly" boring, which arguably could be one reason for the high prevalence of traffic accidents among young men in the military – the quest for excitement when the chance arises. And far from possibly producing a developmental opportunity, it was argued that such early participation (around age 18) in the military clearly had a detrimental effect on emotional intelligence: if young men were required to do military service, it was suggested that it should be on completion of their education.

The international review team remained unaware of any possibilities for conscientious objection (or what the consequences might be)[17] or any alternative of civilian

---

17. Documents revealed more details. The term of military service is normally 26 months. The Defence Act of 1992 recognises conscientious objection on ethical, moral, humanitarian, philosophical, political or religious grounds, but the alternative offered is a very long period of non-armed service: either 34 months in uniform in army precincts or 42 months without uniform outside army precincts. These regulations do not match the standards of the Council of Europe. Legislation is contemplated to make Cypriot law compatible with the Recommendations on the subject by the Committee of Ministers (Council of Europe, Report by Mr Alvaro Gil-Robles, Commissioner for Human Rights, on his visit to Cyprus, 25-29 June, 2003, para. 45, p. 12).

service. It was suggested the latter could still contribute to 'border' issues, but represent a gesture towards the demilitarisation of society and thereby perhaps one step towards prospective unification.

Cyprus is a highly militarised society and there is a ubiquitous presence of soldiers, more so in the north. There are the peace-keeping UNOP personnel in the demilitarised zone, 40 000 Turkish and Turkish Cypriot troops and 20 000 Greek Cypriot troops in Cyprus – it is one of the most militarised sectors in the world. This inevitably colours everything that goes on in Cyprus and is a daily reminder of the Cyprus Problem as individuals go about their everyday lives. That naturally affects the psyche of young people, all the more so when they are actively engaged in military service. The international review team feels it would be inappropriate to comment specifically on this matter, though its more general views are scattered throughout this report.

4.1.10. The church

In an increasingly secular Europe, the church (or, more precisely, the influence of religion) is often a somewhat peripheral factor in 'youth policy', either in influencing it or supporting it. The exception, in the Council of Europe international reviews of national youth policy undertaken to date, has been Malta (see Evans 2003). It was difficult, however, to distil exactly how the (Greek Orthodox) church affects youth policy. It was reported that

> "The religious element is still dominant, though it is not like the Catholic Church which tries to affect directly law making and policies. But the Church does overshadow our job." (draft National Report, Culture chapter, p. 31)

This last point was a reference to sex education and women's empowerment in relation to self-determination. By and large, however, the international review team gained the impression that, while the Greek Orthodox Church has a continuing spiritual role, it is equally a social forum within local community life. The international review team learned little about the presence and place of other religions, including Islam. Yet, in recent years in many parts of the world, space has been created for inter-religious dialogue and inter-denominational communication; the international review team was told that such practice has taken place in Cyprus too, though only by youth organisations that are "not currently involved in the system". There is potential for this to be developed, though it is still only at a very embryonic stage.

Recommendation 18:

The international review team is aware that inter-religious dialogue in many parts of the world can represent a powerful platform for peace education and intercultural learning. In Cyprus it could also be a basis for the promotion of tolerance and understanding.

4.2. Key issues for youth policy

4.2.1. Participation and citizenship

One of the mantras of young people throughout Europe, when arguing for and advocating participation in decision-making and opportunities to engage in active citizenship, is "Nothing about us without us". This has produced interminable debates about the meanings of 'participation' and 'citizenship' (which are related, but certainly not identical ideas – and can be different).[18] It has also raised questions about the nature of representation, which may be 'democratic' or 'categorical', or something else (see Williamson 2002).

The involvement of young people in structures of decision-making invariably leads to a need to reconsider hierarchies of power and 'traditional' forms of power and control. People do not give up power and control readily: in Cyprus, the point was made to the international review team, in its meeting with the intra-departmental consultative committee, that a recent evaluation report had suggested involving students more closely in the governance of schooling – "but this was politically contentious; there are very strong teachers' associations in Cyprus". Yet, at a national level, the Cyprus Youth Board is committed to developing a 'Youth Parliament':

"This specific project aims at bringing Cyprus Youth closer to involvement in social issues of common interest in a similar way to the 'Parliament of Adolescents' which is successfully implemented in Greece. This will be achieved through the organising of a two-day seminar with the participation of about 100 young people under 25 from all organised youth bodies in Cyprus. This project will be implemented in collaboration with the Ministry of Education, the House of Representatives and the Cyprus Youth Board, and aims at submitting to these competent authorities the proposals approved by the 'Youth Parliament' regarding the various problems which concern youth. Following last year's first successful meeting of the 'Youth Parliament' the Cyprus Youth Organisation aims at organising a second one in 2004 with the participation of young Turkish-Cypriots also." (Budget 2004, p. 39)

Such a statement might have something of a hollow ring for those youth organisations that feel the Cyprus Youth Board itself does not give sufficient attention or recognition to those youth organisations that are not firmly connected to the mainstream political establishment. Indeed, the international review team was told that the reason so many young people were members of political youth organisations was because this was the only way to secure effective influence for youth. However, recent research conducted by the Cyprus Youth Board[19] suggests that young people's interest and involvement in politics is less widespread than the international review team had been led to believe in face-to-face encounters. Two-thirds of the young were hardly interested in politics at all, and only 12% were very interested. Moreover, the research revealed that just 15% of young people belonged to a political organisation – and therefore 85% did not.

This compares to findings from another research study where over half of young people were members of at least one organised youth group, a category which included political groups, but also athletic clubs and voluntary and professional associations. Significantly perhaps, that study noted that the "politicisation of the

___

18. This became starkly evident at the Students' Forum 2000 meeting in the Czech Republic in 2002: one of those attending had been very active in his own country on the question of 'youth participation' and, as a result of his activism, had been stripped of national citizenship. 'Citizenship' is, of course, now considered in 'multidimensional' ways and is no longer restricted to ideas of nationality and the possession of a passport.

19. Research on matters that concern the free time of Cypriot youth, employment problems, relationships, beliefs and the problems of youth, Cyprus Youth Board, 2002.

groups" was second only to "shortage of time" as a reason stated for not belonging to an organised group (Dr E. Demetriades, "Survey on the active participation of youth in Cypriot society", 2001, p. 7). This may be some indication that young people are gradually becoming disenchanted with the nature of Cypriot politics, just as most young people elsewhere have become disillusioned with mainstream politics across the political spectrum.

'Co-management' is a central principle of the Council of Europe's Youth Directorate and its work, which is informed by the CDEJ, representing member governments, and an Advisory Council, representing youth organisations. The Cyprus Youth Board prides itself on a similar approach and identified this as an example of good practice to recommend to other countries:

> "The way the Youth Board operates (co-management system) is an example of participation of the young in Decision making on matters that concern them. The General Advisory Body (combining the political committee, the students committee and the trade union committee) advise the Administrative Board, which is responsible for letting the Ministry of Justice know about the problems that concern the young people of Cyprus." (Cyprus Youth Board response to EU White Paper questionnaire on participation, p. 8)

Given the concerns expressed earlier in this report about the place of non-political youth organisations in this structure and about the status of a 'National Youth Council', such claims have to be treated with some caution.

But the claims concerning youth participation go even further and cement, at least rhetorically, the commitment of Cyprus to involving young people in all aspects of governance on questions affecting them:

> "The young people should be involved in the decisions which concern them because they are able to make the right choices in the matters that really have an impact in their lives. Also young people learn to be interested and to get involved in problems that other young people face at that time, which in the future might become problems of their own.
>
> The Administrative Board of the Youth Board of Cyprus, the Advisory Body, the National Youth Council, the Parliament of the Young people and the Parliament of the Teenagers act as advisers on matters that concern them." (Cyprus Youth Board response to EU White Paper questionnaire on participation, p. 8)

Such a presentation of the situation gives an impression of equity in the advisory contribution across the bodies mentioned, which is clearly not the case. Nevertheless, despite the sometimes vocal criticisms of the disproportionate political control perceived to be exercised within the Youth Board, there was still ultimately a pervasive belief that Cyprus was moving in the right direction. Few condemned the Youth Board out of hand and many advocated a need to, for example "sustain and further enhance the role of the Youth Board of Cyprus" (Cyprus Youth Board, "Proposal on youth social involvement", p. 6). The board has certainly been instrumental in pioneering innovative approaches to youth participation, not least in the area of the municipal youth councils, though to date there are only eight (or nine) in operation. These need to be expanded and 'upgraded', to allow "young people who do not belong to an organised youth group to participate" (ibid., p. 16). In short, the Cyprus Youth Board has been a powerful driver of youth participation but, in this process, has exposed practice that demands reflection and attention.

Recommendation 19:

The international review team believes that the principles of youth participation in Cyprus are well articulated and that the basis for good practice has been established. This now needs to be consolidated and developed – and particular attention given to some legitimate criticisms concerning the place and voice of less organised and less politicised young people.

Beyond the issue of young people's participation in the formal structures of administration, there is the question of their 'social involvement' and opportunities to exercise practical citizenship within the context of civil society. It has been argued that at one time nation-states had to 'make' their young people; now it is for young people to 'make' the new Europe and the societies in which they live (Lauritzen and Guidikova 2002). In Finland, the rationale underpinning youth policy is that young people have a responsibility to make the most of the opportunities available, but the government has to ensure that there is a framework within which such opportunities are available (see Williamson 1999, 2002). Social involvement is a vital part of such a framework of opportunities and, indeed, is one of the topics on which the Cyprus Youth Board is currently consulting with young people.

A recent survey conducted by the Cyprus Family Planning Association found that only 17% of young people claimed to be members of volunteer organisations, though six in ten young people claimed an interest in becoming volunteers (Cyprus Family Planning Association, Presentation on volunteerism, pp. 8-9). The Cyprus Youth Board has argued that:

"Volunteers in Cyprus feel that voluntary activities offer them a sense of self-fulfilment. They feel that the experiences acquired through participation in voluntary organisations contribute to their social and personal development, are unique in kind and will have a lifelong impact on the development of the individual's personality. Volunteerism, as a form of participation in public life, strengthens the socialisation of young people and stimulates their benign interests for their fellow beings.

Moreover, volunteers have mentioned that their involvement in public and social life has contributed to their physical and mental health; volunteerism has encouraged them to exercise and read more; and has prevented many of them from smoking, using drugs or reacting violently to tense situations. Hence, volunteerism has a positive impact on their journey through life as it contributes to their appreciation of life and impels them to capture the real essence of life, away from vain and conceited pursuits." (Cyprus Youth Board response to EU White Paper questionnaire on voluntary activities, p. 12)

Yet the infrastructure for volunteering and social involvement in Cyprus remains fragile. There are no special regulations to protect volunteers, a 'lack of formal acknowledgement by the state', limited training opportunities and generally an absence of recognition. This does not mean, however, that volunteering is an 'invisible' pursuit. Although experience of social involvement is given relatively little weight in the labour market, it is recognised by universities when applying for undergraduate and graduate programmes. Voluntary activities are also 'governed' by the Pan-Cyprian Welfare Council, which has some forty members, usually associations with a specific concern for particular vulnerable groups, but including the Scouts and Guides. The Cyprus Youth Board sees the importance of strengthening support for young people interested in engaging in voluntary work (see Budget 2004, p. 36), and there appears to be widespread support for doing so (for example, Intercultural Centre of Cyprus, "Proposal for the development of a national youth policy of Cyprus" on the theme 'of social involvement'; and "Proposal on youth social involvement").

Only at Apanemi, the Women's Information and Support Centre, did the international review team encounter a sophisticated reflection on the 'challenge' of volunteering – in terms of information provision ('advertising'), recruitment, training, support and appropriate engagement according to the organisational needs, personal skills and motivation of the prospective volunteers. Such a strategic framework, in order to maximise the potential of 'social involvement' for society and individuals, is a key focus of 'youth policy' thinking elsewhere in Europe.[20] The ground seems to be fertile in Cyprus for giving attention to a more integrated and purposeful 'volunteering' strategy – in the interests of both youth participation and social citizenship.

Recommendation 20:

The international review team notes the increasing interest and commitment in Cyprus to the 'active engagement' and 'social involvement' of young people. It also notes, however, the absence of a coherent framework for such development. It recommends, therefore, that consideration should be given to a more robust strategy for volunteering, in the interests of both 'hosting' organisations and presenting volunteers, drawing on models already in existence elsewhere in Europe.

Finally, the international review team was interested in the potential for representation and participation by 'minority' groups of young people, such as young people with disabilities or gay, lesbian and bisexual young people. Throughout the international review team's two visits to the island, such groups (which are often prominent elsewhere) were conspicuous by their absence. The Cyprus Youth Board informed the team that there were 41 'youth organisations' for disability and illness, some run by such young people and some run for them. There was not, however, even one youth organisation dedicated to the needs of young people with alternative sexual orientations, though there was one organisation for gay men of all ages.

Recommendation 21:

The international review team feels that the Cyprus Youth Board and others need to give greater attention to the specific needs of 'minority' groups of young people, such as those with disabilities or those with alternative sexual orientation.

---

20. Following the European Commission's 1995 White Paper on Teaching and Learning, the EVS (European Voluntary Service) Programme was established. This sets out clear guidelines for good practice in relation to both hosting and sending organisations, in order to provide appropriate support to the young people involved. Similar guidelines are in place for national initiatives such as 'Millennium Volunteers' in the United Kingdom.

Dimensions of youth policy

4.2.2. Combating social exclusion and promoting inclusion

The international review team gained little sense of issues concerning the 'social exclusion' of young people as this is conventionally understood elsewhere. There were fleeting references to "gypsy" children (especially girls) dropping out of school prematurely, but otherwise the impression gained was of a youth population who were largely included – in their families and in education. This seemed, however, to be an implicit and exclusive reference to young Greek Cypriots. The international review team heard almost nothing about the situation and circumstances of young people from either the three established minority religious groups (who are aligned with the Greek Cypriots and probably have similar life trajectories, though in their own distinct ways) or new immigrant populations (engaged possibly in sex work, labouring or the tourist trade). Moreover, if the drugs problem is as bad as routinely suggested, this is a key factor leading to personal exclusion as well as the corrosion of local communities.

Given that social inclusion is a paramount objective of youth policy in many other European countries, which recurrently express concern about 'exclusion', 'marginalisation' and 'drop-out', the international review team felt compelled to ask: does exclusion not exist in Cyprus, or is it just unseen? In other words, does Cyprus still have no need to address such challenges? Even if this is so, it is unlikely that Cyprus will remain immune from such challenges, for they are pervasive across Europe. It may be, however, that such challenges are already there and that they were simply not brought with any force to the attention of the international review team.

Certainly in the Intercultural Centre's submission to the Cyprus Youth Board on one of its consultation themes, there was a section dedicated to the question of social inclusion and robust advocacy of the initiatives required:

"Action towards social inclusion should address youth that due to complicated factors, with a negative influence on their lives and personal development, are facing the danger of social exclusion. Dysfunctional families, poverty, school drop-out, juvenile behaviour, physical or mental disability, are some of the reasons that may put youth at risk of social exclusion. In many cases social exclusion may begin at an early age (abused children that are caught up in a vicious cycle of violence when they are adults) or at puberty (juvenile delinquency).

The state has the responsibility for developing a strong policy to combat the root factors that lead to social exclusion. Action towards social inclusion should put an emphasis on education, creative occupation, social support, employment, combating violence and any form of abuse, supporting rehabilitation from substance abuse etc." (Intercultural Centre of Cyprus, "Proposal for the development of a national youth policy of Cyprus" on the themes of 'Equality, human rights, social inclusion and intercultural dialogue', p. 2)

The proposal goes on to list seven discrete areas in which such a 'social inclusion' strategy might be developed. The international review team is aware of various initiatives which, at least in part, already contribute to such objectives: the ZEP school, Apanemi, KENTHEA and the emerging work of the Anti-Drugs Council. Once again, however, an overarching framework appears to be lacking. Elsewhere in Europe, attention is now turning away from focused or positive action directed at specific 'minority' or 'disadvantaged' groups, towards overarching concepts of 'access' and 'inclusion'. In other words, policy is focused on enabling individuals to take advantage of opportunities available and ensuring there are no inappropriate barriers preventing individuals from doing so. Access by Turkish Cypriot youth NGOs to the European YOUTH programme is a stark case in point, and the Cyprus Youth Board has already expressed its intention to remove the obstacles, as far as it possibly can (see above).

Recommendation 22:

The international review team recommends a more thorough scrutiny to ensure that access to a range of constructive social opportunities is not obstructed, for particular social groups of young people, by barriers which may not be readily apparent to the 'dominant mind'. Only through so doing will the risks of increasing levels of social exclusion, especially among more marginal and disadvantaged groups, be minimised.

4.2.3. Youth information

The Youth Information Centres in Nicosia and Larnaca are impressive and arguably world-class. They appear to be well-used by diverse groups of young people, who are naturally attracted by free access to computers and the Internet, but who also benefit from the personal (and very personable) engagement of the staff. There are plans to establish three other such centres in the major cities in Cyprus, four regional information centres and two information points.[21] The Cyprus Youth Board also provides information on substance misuse through its anti-drugs helpline, which has been in operation since 1990 and was the first helpline ever to address substance-related issues in Cyprus. The objective is for all young people in Cyprus to have access to extensive, up-to-date and reliable information on all issues about which they are concerned or interested.

Apart from the anti-drugs helpline, the youth information field in Cyprus is relatively new, with the oldest youth information centre being operational for no more than two years. Best practice is being developed, with plans to include youth advice structures (counselling centres) within the youth information centres.

Any youth information and advice service needs a process by which information is gathered and 'checked' before it is disseminated. The process in Cyprus is described as follows:

"The information addressed to young people is disseminated through the Youth Information Centres. The information reaches the centres as a result of a close collaboration with governmental organisations as well as NGOs that specialise in youth matters. Therefore, any source of information is firstly checked by the youth workers with regard to the status, objectives and topics covered, before any co-operation is established for the gathering of informative material." (Cyprus Youth Board, response to the EU White Paper questionnaire on information, p. 7)

---

21. In its Budget proposals for 2004, the Cyprus Youth Board seeks resources to support youth information centres in Nicosia, Larnaca, Paphos, Agros, Akaki and Polemidia. It also seeks notional resources to negotiate the development of district centres in Limassol and Paralimni, and regional centres in Ora and Polemi (Budget 2004, p. 22). All this youth information development is being developed in partnership with other authorities, in order to share the burden of its considerable cost.

Dimensions of youth policy

It was not clear, however, quite how this 'checking' by the youth workers was done. In other places, it is often done by means of a formally constituted 'ethics committee', which evaluates information for 'accuracy, balance and fairness' before it is made available for young people.

Recommendation 23:

The international review team would suggest, as youth information services proliferate in Cyprus, that a formal national 'ethics committee' be constituted in order to ensure that the information made available through leaflets or through any on-line service is validated for its accuracy, balance and fairness.

Nor was the international review team able to establish the nature of demand for youth information services. It was reported that there had been some 600 enquiries on the drugs helpline, but there was no indication that these had been analysed to determine the nature of enquiries or the outcomes of advice provided. Similarly, it was not apparent that any analysis had yet been done of the use by young people of youth information centres, despite the claim that:

"Statistics that are kept at the Youth Information Centres enable the evaluation of the provision of information to young people. These statistics of the young visitors are collected on a monthly basis and are then analysed with respect to the issues on which information is requested. The evaluation for each centre is then used to enrich the information material and enhance the flow of information within the centres. There are plans for the drawing up of a questionnaire to be given to the young visitors of the centres requesting their opinion on the information provided and other feedback regarding information." (Cyprus Youth Board, response to the EU White Paper questionnaire on information, p. 2)

The international review team has little doubt that such an evaluation would yield very positive results. Youth information centres were among the few places where there was living evidence of services being used by young people from diverse ethnic backgrounds. Nevertheless, there appears to be an urgent need for a critical appraisal of both the kinds of young people making use of youth information centres and the reasons they are doing so. There may, then, also be a need to explore why some groups of young people may not be making use of the facility. In other countries, similar provision has had to recognise that factors such as location, perceptions of users and styles of practice can act as barriers to engagement with such services. Youth information services need to connect with the cultural and physical pathways of young people, as the draft National Report notes:

"A final concern (and suggestion) addresses the decentralisation and cultural profile of the Youth Information Centres. Large groups of young people in Nicosia, for example, still ignore the existence of the Youth Information Centre located on Makariou avenue, a few metres down the road from the Hilton hotel. The familiarity of young people with and their usage of these centres are not, unfortunately, corresponding to the number and excellent quality of facilities, information and support such centres provide...

The Cyprus Youth Board, like all of us, needs to learn how to use economies and channels of popular culture in order to activate the trafficking of other cultures. A supplementary strategy towards this direction would be that opening of peripheral Youth Information Centres in places which already constitute youth crossroads or cultural posts for young people. The Ledras Palas checkpoint on the buffer zone, the University of Cyprus, the Cineplex are perhaps not neutral places but nevertheless youth hubs where information booths could function as interfaces between information and youth flows." (draft National Report, Culture chapter, p. 35)

These are powerful and useful observations, reinforcing the case for knowing how young people are currently making use of youth information services and thus informing the way a more sophisticated system – with reach and relevance – might be developed.

Recommendation 24:

The international review team recommends an early exploration of the types of young people making use of youth information provision, and the reasons they are doing so. Despite their evident strengths and qualities, this would provide an 'early warning' system for addressing any emergent challenges or problems.

Access to, and sometimes guidance on, information has become a critical feature of modern life,[22] not just for young people. One of the central complaints and concerns among the young people in Kato Pyrgos was their lack of access to information. Youth information services in Cyprus are in an early stage of development, but an ambitious programme of expansion is proposed and is to be welcomed. It is firmly supported by the government, one of whose core aims for youth policy is 'to ensure the right of young people to information through the expansion and completion of the programme regarding the establishment of Youth Information Centres, all over Cyprus' (Governance Programme of Mr Tassos Papadopoulos, President of the Republic of Cyprus, p. 1).

4.2.4. Multiculturalism and minorities

The enlarging Europe has witnessed a dramatic increase in mobility and migration, and a corresponding increasing presence of minorities in what were, until quite recently, largely monocultural communities. Despite the richness that such multicultural exchange can afford, it also poses challenges around combating racism and xenophobia, and promoting intercultural tolerance and understanding. This is a central platform of the work of the Council of Europe, particularly within the Youth Directorate.

In Cyprus, such issues tend to be overwhelmed by the Cyprus Problem and the relationships between Greek and Turkish Cypriots, who are physically divided by the partition of the island, worsened by the extensive presence of Turkish settlers and Turkish troops in the north. And, though the children of Turkish settlers born on the island are constitutionally Cypriots, many struggle to define their own identity; indeed, they have been described as a 'lost generation' – neither Cypriot nor Anatolian. Furthermore, the international review team was told that some young

---

22. At the Students' Forum 2000 in Prague in 1999, which explored 'values for education in a globalising world', one working group of students came up with the concept of 'FREUD'. In a world of information overload, the most critical challenge for education was to enable young people to develop a capacity and competence to Find, Retrieve, Evaluate, Use and Defend the material that informed the pathways of their lives.

Cypriots from settler families in the north were indistinguishable from 'cross-generational' young Cypriots. In contrast, others lived in what were described as 'Turkish ghettos', their parents having arrived en bloc as part of a whole community from Anatolia, transplanting their customs and traditions, which they have sustained in Cyprus.

And, apart from settler children born in Cyprus, the Turkish Cypriot authorities have since 1975 adopted a policy of 'naturalisation' for immigrants from Turkey, which 'constitutes a further barrier to a peaceful negotiated solution of the Cypriot conflict' (Council of Europe, Parliamentary Assembly, "The demographic structure of Cyprus", April 1992, p. 24). The demographic position in the north is therefore extremely complex, a point confirmed in a report which made further distinctions between categories of settlers (such as managers and peasants). The report expressed concern, for a range of reasons, about illegal, undeclared Turkish workers, to whom 'the authorities were shutting their eyes' (ibid., p. 15). There are also the 'enclaved' Greek Cypriots in the north of the island, in the Karpas peninsula region. Their freedom of religious expression and freedom of movement, including access to Greek Cypriot secondary education, have been violated (Council of Europe, Report by Mr Alvaro Gil-Robles, Commissioner of Human Rights, on his visit to Cyprus, 25-29 June 2003).

Beyond these issues, there are questions about the three 'minor religious groups' aligned to the Greek Cypriots: the Armenians, the Latins and the Maronites (in sum, about 3.4% of all Cypriots). There are also new waves of immigrants, still relatively small in number, but who nevertheless have transformed the ethnic composition of what 'used to be a very closed society'. The population of Cyprus now includes people from Lebanon, Palestine, the Philippines, Sri Lanka, Indonesia, Romania, Ukraine, Bulgaria and Russia. There are bona fide students from abroad, 'students' claiming asylum and access to the European Union, the migrant partners of Cypriots, expatriates and 'gypsies'. The international review team heard very little discussion of any of these groups, almost as if they lived in 'parallel worlds'.

Research conducted by the Cyprus Youth Board[23] was said to have 'proved that intolerance and prejudice among Cypriot young people is a fact' (Budget 2004, p. 34). This has led the youth board to promote a number of programmes and campaigns directed towards combating prejudice and discrimination, including a Rainbow Festival, which seeks to involve young people from all ethnic groups in Cyprus. Other measures purportedly addressing the challenge of multiculturalism have been implemented in other parts of the administration. For example, just under 5% of pupils attending public primary schools do not speak Greek as their mother tongue.

In response, there are new policies for the distribution of such pupils across districts, schools and even classrooms and for the provision of additional language support 'so that teachers can support their linguistic and cultural needs more effectively':

> "Multicultural education is currently being practised in Cyprus in the form of various support measures. These measures can be categorised as measures for language support, which refer to the learning of Greek as a second language and measures for facilitating the smooth integration of groups with different cultural identities." (reported in draft National Report, Culture chapter, p. 20)

23 . Cyprus Youth Board, "Youth of Cyprus – free time, work, relationships, perceptions and problems", 2002.

This approach to 'multiculturalism' was depicted by some as 'one-way traffic', in contrast to the celebrated educational programme organised by the Cyprus Youth Board to promote 'cultural consciousness'. Cyprus-Aegean, Myth-History-Art started in 2001 and has been described as 'unique' and 'ground-breaking', especially for its approach, which emphasises 'processes of translation, exchange, influence and transculturation, rather than Civilisations as the testaments of nation states' (draft National Report, Culture chapter, p. 22). In the view of the international review team, this kind of programme, along with the kinds of initiatives being taken by the ZEP school in Limassol, are the starting point for addressing 'difference' in ways that promote respect, rather than disdain, for the 'other'.

Recommendation 25:

The Council of Europe has a long track record in the development of materials for intercultural learning and human rights education. These should be used for supporting the emergent desire in Cyprus to respond positively to the relatively new challenges it faces in terms of its increasingly multicultural population.

Notwithstanding the continuing tensions and difficulties between the Greek Cypriot and Turkish Cypriot communities, the Republic of Cyprus Government has formally recorded its intention, through the Office for Turkish Cypriot Affairs, to

"Co-ordinate state efforts for the careful scrutiny of all legislation, political and administrative practices in order to avoid discrimination against Turkish Cypriots in their implementation." (Republic of Cyprus, Memorandum, Government Policy vis-à-vis The Turkish Cypriots (Set of Measures), 30 April 2003, p. 4)

The Bi-Communal Youth Forum, comprising youth organisations from both the north and the south of the island, has already produced a number of 'common declarations'. Clearly, there are also youth organisations outside this consensus, yet the international review team did not find any dramatic divergence from the Youth Forum's aspirations

- To continue the struggle for the promotion of co-operation and peaceful co-existence among the youth and people of Cyprus in both communities (2002)
- [To promote] peace and reconciliation and fostering co-operation between Greek Cypriots and Turkish Cypriots … the certainty that the time will come when our people will be able to work, live and fight together in a concerted effort to build the future for our children, in a peaceful and prosperous Federal Cyprus (2003).

The international review team felt the climate was right – with Cyprus in the EU – to support closer links between youth organisations from north and south of the island, in order to build stronger intercultural understanding and a shared Cypriot identity within a wider Europe.

4.2.5. Mobility and internationalism

The people of Cyprus have always been a highly mobile and international population with historically high levels of emigration. Today, the character of that mobility is very different, particularly the scale of young Cypriots studying abroad and Turkish Cypriots from the north of the island leaving for good. Now that Cyprus is a member of the European Union, there is the question of even stronger engagement with European programmes aimed at young people. Indeed, this was the main focus of young people's discussions with the international review team – though young people sometimes confused us with the European Commission and sought our help in tackling technical problems with the YOUTH programme!

Responses to membership of the EU were somewhat mixed. Having freed itself from the shackles of British colonialism in 1960, there was still some reticence in Cyprus about becoming 'answerable' to Brussels (a version of the 'from Moscow to Brussels' perspective among some in former communist countries that have also just joined the EU). The main concern was higher taxes, and the 'minority' representation of Cyprus within the European Parliament (just 6 MEPs out of 724). On the plus side, the international review team was told that Cypriots wanted to adopt some of the institutional and cultural practices of the European Union – human rights, educational reform, advance to the knowledge society.

The international review team heard from individuals and organisations involved in a range of European programmes, not just the YOUTH programme, but also Erasmus and Socrates. All pointed to the positive experiences of that involvement. Taking part had 'changed our way of thinking', 'helped us to understand the way of life of other people' or 'made me aware of the power of non-formal education'. One youth organisation concerned with environmental (coastline) protection has joined a network of similarly-focused youth organisations from a number of countries. And whereas participation by young people in Cyprus in the 'Youth for Europe' programme (which ran until 1997) had been limited, there were now about 800 Cypriots participating in youth exchanges. The European Voluntary Service (EVS) programme was, in contrast, rather under-subscribed, which was attributed to military service for young men and the need to defer the pursuance of formal studies.

The international review team was alerted to two particular issues with mobility and internationalism arising from engagement with opportunities in Europe. One was to level the playing field in terms of access to these programmes for Cypriots in the north – for example, no EVS volunteers could be 'hosted' in the north, for insurance and other reasons. Travel logistics and costs were also a problem, though much the same arguments could be made for young people living in Paphos. Although these were sometimes technical issues, their impact worked against the full potential for participation in these programmes by Turkish Cypriots.

Recommendation 26:

The international review team felt that the European Commission, in consultation with the national agency for Cyprus, and the Cyprus Youth Board, should explore how best to overcome barriers to participation in EU youth programmes for Turkish Cypriots and thereby provide as equal an opportunity as possible for all Cypriots, irrespective of their place of residence.

Secondly, despite the very positive experiences described by individual young people, the international review team was concerned about the potential for 'cascading' those learning benefits to other young people in Cyprus. There did not appear to be any 'network infrastructure' to enable young people who have participated in international programmes to capitalise further on their learning and development, perhaps by collaborating on 'mirror-image' initiatives in Cyprus. Further, this could give added value by strengthening a platform for non-political youth activity and organisation, and thereby add to the possibility of building a more vibrant civil society.

Recommendation 27:

The international review team believes that, as young Cypriots take an increasing part in a variety of European youth programmes, a 'network infrastructure' needs to be established, so that they can both consolidate and disseminate the learning they have gained.

4.2.6. Equal opportunities

Many issues of equal opportunities have already been discussed in this report, not least in relation to questions of access and inclusion. The international review team had to try to get 'underneath' the official position and formal legislation (as one has to do in most countries, for few are explicitly discriminatory any more – though there are exceptions). The team was told repeatedly that the legislative framework often meant very little: it was either lip service or it was ignored. This may be a blunt allegation, but it was clear that Cyprus is a highly formalised and structured society which, certainly in some areas of life, serves to conceal a rather different cultural underbelly. Domestic violence against women, for example, remains widespread, according to a number of respondents, though women are increasingly asserting their autonomy and rights. The automatic withdrawal of driving licences from those exempted from military service for "psychological reasons" (a euphemism for homosexual tendencies) has been condemned as "plainly unreasonable" by the Human Rights Commissioner of the Council of Europe. Furthermore, the real meaning of this description is known to all and therefore disadvantages such people in their occupational and social life.

In terms of gender equality, the key driver in Cyprus is the National Machinery for Women's Rights (NMWR) within the Ministry of Justice and Public Order. Most representative women's organisations participate in the NMWR, which advises the Council of Ministers on issues related to equality. In its response to the EU youth White Paper questionnaire on participation, the Cyprus Youth Board went into considerable detail on current mechanisms for securing equality between women and men. That submission concluded by observing that:

> "The fact that all political parties have increased the number of women candidates which has reached the number of 85 (compared to 32 in 1991 and 55 in 1996) as well as the fact that the elections of the 27th of May 1991 resulted in a 100% increase (from 3 to 6) in women MPs elected has justified the efforts of the National Machinery of Women's Rights." (Cyprus Youth Board response to EU White Paper questionnaire on participation)

Nevertheless, with the exception of its contact with the children's home in Limassol and the Women's Information and Support Centre, the international review team could not help observing that positions in most structures (certainly at the higher levels) continued to be dominated by men. Clearly, change is in progress and Cypriot society is in a process of evolution. The international review team hopes that the Cyprus Youth Board will ensure that it keeps pace with such developments by complying fully with one of its central objects:

"To provide equal opportunities to all young people and their organisations for participation and assumption of responsibility in the social, economic and cultural development and progress of their community and the country in general." (The Youth Board Law, para. 6(b), p. 3)

5. Supporting youth policy

In the first seven Council of Europe international reviews of national youth policy, it became evident that effective youth policy was built on a pyramid of youth research, appropriate training and the dissemination of 'good practice'.

5.1. Youth research

The draft National Report indicates that there is already a strong body of research evidence on many fronts, for example: the prevalence of drug misuse, types of offending behaviour or levels of qualification. This report has made use of very detailed survey findings in relation to substance misuse and the social involvement of young people. The Cyprus Youth Board has also commissioned and produced the following research studies:

- Leisure time of youth
- The problems of repatriated Cypriot youth
- School drop-outs
- Juvenile delinquency
- Young people in refugee camps
- The active participation of young people
- Negative influence on young people of violence in the media
- Youth clubs
- Young people and drugs
- Pontians in primary education
- Culture and violent behaviour of children and young people
- Military service
- The abandonment of rural areas and the provision of incentives for employability within the agricultural economy

During 2004, four other studies were to be completed.[24]

- Current infrastructure projects of benefit to young people
- Students' welfare
- Leisure time, work, relationships and concerns
- Youth entrepreneurship

---

24. This information was drawn from a handout listing the research projects completed and in progress, but in the Budget 2004 document there is also mention of a study on 'student assistance'.

The international review team did not have access to all this body of research, but clearly it is a disparate mix. Moreover, there were many areas on which reliable data did not seem to be available. Predictably, much of this related to the situation in the north of Cyprus, where the international review team had to rely on anecdotal 'evidence', apart from the crime chapter of the draft National Report. Given that this report was concerned with all young people in Cyprus, it would have been useful to have had such comparative data, as well as specific data on the religious minorities in the south and minority ethnic groups. The absence of these data meant that the international review team felt it was often being channelled into considering the position of only Greek Cypriot young people. Of more concern, if such data are not available at all, is the basis upon which any rational and 'evidence-based' response can be made to the young people concerned.

There can, of course, be an over-obsession among researchers with the acquisition of data. Sometimes there is too much research and the real issue is the effective delivery of policy. One can always delay action by seeking to discover more before anything is implemented! In policy-making terms, however, the problem is that, even when research has been conducted, it can often be 'data-rich, but information-poor'. In other words, it can blind the reader and the policy maker with statistics, but lacks explanatory power that can guide policy-making. In Cyprus, there appears to be a wealth of research (in some quarters at least), which provides numbers and percentages (distributions and classifications), but considerably less qualitative work that might help to explain and illuminate. The international review team made this point in relation to youth information developments, where both quantitative and qualitative research appears to be needed to inform future progress.

At the heart of these remarks lies the need for a more coherent research strategy and a wider public discussion of the concepts, issues and evidence that are needed to inform a policy-making process. Academic research papers do not always assist such a process; partnership and dialogue between government and researchers (and indeed practitioners) will[25]. The international review team felt that this essential 'triangle' of relationships, which supports a virtuous cycle of youth policy development, has yet to be fully formed in Cyprus.

> **Recommendation 28:**
>
> The international review team believes that the relationships between research, policy and practice need to be strengthened in order to contest and clarify the 'evidence' on which youth policy is constructed.

5.2. Training

Training can take many forms and need not be highly 'professionalised' in a conventional sense. It may take place in house, at the local level and in 'bite-sized' chunks. Alternatively, it can of course be delivered as a substantial module by an educational institution. There is an increasing view, in parts of Europe at least, that there needs to be a common basis of training for all practitioners who work with young people – so that there is a shared understanding of prevailing issues and some shared sense of teaching and learning pedagogies.

---

25. Since the mid-1990s in the UK there has been a 'Research, Policy and Practice Forum on Young People', which interrogates key ideas in the youth policy arena, challenges political assumptions and draws on the experience of practitioners in the delivery of, for example, 'mentoring' or projects designed to enhance 'self-esteem'.

The international review team remained unaware of any professional training infrastructure, beyond the more formal academic and professional training courses available in institutes of higher education and professional development. The review team was concerned about the apparent absence of training for those responsible for delivering programmes, for example, within the network of youth clubs. The team was not told whether those working in youth information centres received any training, but it was told that the services provided to young people in many domains of youth policy were delivered by untrained – and this does not mean uneducated – professionals (for example, social welfare practitioners working with young offenders, or secondary school teachers).

Effective practice depends upon practitioners being clear about their task and about which mechanisms can best achieve it. Only through training programmes can the 'system' be sure that it has prepared people appropriately for their tasks. This approach is the precursor of performance assessment and quality assurance, which can start to establish whether a young person in Kato Pyrgos is getting the same level of access to, and experience of, an initiative or intervention as any other young person in Cyrpus. It is quite bizarre that there is a rigidly prescribed curriculum in the formal education system, whereas beyond it – in what might, in some aspects at least, be crudely described as a non-formal learning arena – it appears that almost anything, and anyone, goes. If drug misuse is to be prevented, youth offending reduced, access to youth information enhanced or European youth opportunities increased, then a training framework for 'youth practitioners' needs to be established. This may contain core modules and various dedicated optional extras (for different types of practitioner), but occasional seminars and well-intentioned voluntary commitment are unlikely to be enough.

Recommendation 29:

The international review team believes that a modest (at first) training framework for those who work with young people across a range of youth policy domains needs to be considered. This would not be concerned with 'high level' professional qualifications (such as counselling or psychology), but with the core components of developing and delivering effective practice, through building relationships and cultivating the motivation of young people.

5.3. The dissemination of good practice

'Best practice' clearly requires the production of credible evaluation but, once such evaluation has taken place, it is important to have mechanisms for sharing concepts, knowledge and methodologies across the field. This cannot be left to chance, if investment in new initiatives is to be maximised. The international review team was privileged to see examples of what it felt represented the best of modern practice in Cyprus, across a spectrum of policy domains: the ZEP school in secondary education, KENTHEA in relation to substance misuse, Apanemi in the context of domestic violence, and the youth information centres. On the other hand, the team was surprised to learn that, though the Open Therapeutic Community (Agia Skepia) has been operational for five and a half years, as yet it has 'no results'. Given the inclination in Cyprus to the need for 'quick success' (a typical political problem everywhere), this came as something of a shock! There is a huge difference between seeking to evaluate a programme almost before it has begun, and letting programmes run without apparently any analysis of emergent data.

Both the ZEP school and the Women's Support and Information Centre were eager to share the lessons of their practice with a wider audience. Both said that at least some senior politicians and decision-makers were receptive to their findings. But these were isolated expressions of such commitment. More generally, the international review team gained a sense that people got on with their jobs in 'splendid isolation', detached even from colleagues engaged in quite similar work. This suggested that there was no explicit 'communication strategy' for sharing and discussing practice – good and not so good! Such strategies have no prescriptive blueprint but, as somebody once remarked, if you are going to re-invent the wheel, make sure it is a round one. There are models of good practice within Cyprus and beyond. What is needed in Cyprus, as elsewhere, is a platform from which such ideas can be disseminated. That platform might be an 'action-focused' magazine or journal, a seminar series or regular regional gatherings but, as 'youth policy' in Cyprus develops, it needs one or more such opportunities.

Recommendation 30:

The international review team believes that an opportunity needs to be created, both within and across substantive areas of youth policy, for policy-makers, researchers and practitioners to share both theoretical and empirical ideas about effective practice. To this end, a 'communication strategy' needs to be formulated.

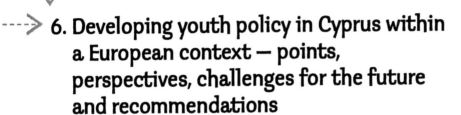

6. Developing youth policy in Cyprus within a European context — points, perspectives, challenges for the future and recommendations

In the development of youth policy, there are a number of reference points available, and these were not available even a few years ago. Not that any of these is fixed; they are simply mechanisms to enable more robust reflection and analysis of a country's current position and also, it is to be hoped, to provide a basis for further adaptation and development, within a country's specific traditions and stage of youth policy development.

6.1. Key principles of the youth work of the Council of Europe

When the first international review of national youth policy took place in Finland in 1997, there were virtually no landmarks or signposts to guide the deliberations of the international review team. As a result, it based its concluding remarks on the four key principles that informed the work of the Youth Directorate in the Council of Europe: participation, co-management, intercultural learning, and an integrated and cross-sectoral approach.

6.1.1. Participation

A key section of this report considers questions of 'participation and citizenship' in Cyprus, and the detailed issues need not be repeated here. Suffice it to say that current philosophies informing the work of the Cyprus Youth Board are a firm step in the right direction. These were expressed clearly within the Youth Board's response to the EU Youth White Paper questionnaire on participation. Nevertheless, the international review team felt that there remained serious questions about the levels of involvement and influence of 'non-political' youth at the levels of both national and municipal governance.

6.1.2. Co-management

This relates closely to questions of participation. The Cyprus Youth Board proclaims that its work is governed and guided by a co-management system – one informed by government (through the consultative intra-departmental committee) and also by youth NGOs (through the Political Committee, the Trade Union body, the Students' Committee and the Advisory Body, which comprises youth organisations from those three committees and others). Yet some considered the weight and balance of influence within this system of co-management to be distorted and unequal, particularly the composition of the Governing/ Administrative Board and the process by which it was appointed. In short, things were considered to be too 'top-down', with insufficient in the way of 'bottom-up' contributions to the loci of decision-making. Hence the controversy about the 'National Youth Council' (see above). Given the will, such issues could be easily resolved – there is widespread support and praise for the work of the Cyprus Youth Board, but the realities of its structures of governance do not persuade everyone that its work is founded on an authentic commitment to 'co-management'.

6.1.3. Intercultural learning

There is much rhetoric in Cyprus about learning from others through cultural exchange, and promoting practice that reflects Cyprus' increasingly multicultural society. The reality seems to be rather different, with the dominant discourse relating to the culture, traditions and aspirations of the Greek Cypriot community while other cultural contexts remain subordinate or, indeed, invisible. The international review team gained glimpses of new, exciting and more progressive approaches and believes that these merit attention in terms of their potential for joining the mainstream of contemporary practice with young people. There is certainly a wealth of international experience on which Cyprus could draw.

6.1.4. Integrated, cross-sectoral policy and practice

Politically and administratively it is always easier to work inside a well-defined departmental framework, where the boundaries of responsibility are clearly understood. In terms of the needs of young people, however, working within such 'silos' is relatively ineffective, for their needs inevitably cross such boundaries. Young offenders, for example, may demand a 'criminal justice' response, but they are also likely to require an 'educational' response and perhaps one which attends to their presenting 'health' problems (often around mental health and drug misuse). The Cyprus Youth Board has already pioneered a range of 'cross-sectoral' working practice, through its partnerships with municipalities, the anti-drugs council and the formal educational system; the international review team believes these are models to be nurtured. The challenge in the future will be to agree the lead body and delineate its remit, rather than unilaterally asserting exclusive responsibility for an area of practice, and to ensure appropriate communication channels where such areas overlap.

6.2. Youth policy indicators

Contrary to the view of the draft National Report (Culture chapter), which alleges that the Council of Europe's Youth Policy Indicators Report (Council of Europe 2003a) is some kind of 'burden' or straitjacket within which youth policy is to be evaluated, the indicators are literally indicative of issues against which youth policy development may be tested and judged. They are designed to enable a measured reflection of progress over time. If policies have been effective, then key positive indicators (such as levels of educational achievement, or access to new technologies) should have improved, while key negative indicators (such as levels of teenage pregnancy, or the prevalence of drug misuse) should have diminished.

The indicators report is publicly available and could provide an internal device for the authorities in Cyprus to reflect on the impact of new youth policy initiatives. Alternatively, given the specificities of youth policy challenges in Cyprus, the

Cypriot authorities might wish to construct their own 'list of indicators'. It is certainly premature to 'test' the current state of play in Cyprus against the published indicators report – and the international review team did not receive the relevant data to do so, in many policy domains – but this should be one basis for considering youth policy development in the future and refining it accordingly.

6.3. The five "C"s

An even cruder, but nonetheless useful, way of thinking about youth policy emerged from the synthesis report of the first seven international reviews of national youth policy (see Williamson 2002). Unlike the 'indicator' approach, which largely uses quantitative signposts, the five 'C's (or at least four of them) are designed to stimulate qualitative debate about whether 'youth policy' is doing what it has been intended to do.

6.3.1. Coverage

The coverage issue is significantly about reach. It has three sub-components: geography, social groups and issues. To give some examples:

- There may be plenty of youth policy access and opportunity in major urban centres, but what about young people in rural areas? Without attention to this issue, social divisions may be increased rather than access equalised.

- New youth policy opportunities are often taken up more readily by young people who are already relatively advantaged in a society. If this persists, then the divide between the haves and have-nots becomes wider – often precisely the opposite outcome to that intended by the provision of new policy.

- Certain youth policy issues may (for a range of reasons) end up being delivered to those who need it least. Drugs education in schools, for example, may be directed at young people who are least likely to use drugs in the first place, whereas drugs intervention programmes outside school can target those most at risk.

Resource decisions always affect the balance and distribution of 'youth policy' measures, but these are nonetheless important questions for consideration. The attention given to young people in rural areas (through, for example, the network of youth clubs and the proposed establishment of information points) in Cyprus is to be commended. There are few 'easy answers' to this question of coverage, but it is an issue that merits regular reflection.

6.3.2. Capacity

Capacity refers to the infrastructure through which policy filters into practice. It is relatively easy to produce a policy document, setting out aspirations, rationale and target groups. It is something else to ensure that policy converts into effective practice, through governmental or non-governmental mechanisms, or a combination of the two. Whereas, in Cyprus, there appears to be a strong centralised lead on a range of youth policy matters (largely, though not exclusively, through the Youth Board), the delivery mechanisms were less clear to the international review team. 'Making things happen' is always a challenge for youth policy. There were useful

issues and themes

73

models – such as Apanemi (an NGO), KENTHEA (an umbrella body) or the ZEP school (a 'community hub' as well as an educational establishment) – on which to build a more robust infrastructure, within and beyond the apparatus of the state.

6.3.3. Competence

The essential aspect of 'making things happen' in youth policy is the quality of the people at the interface between policy aspirations and the young people themselves. Without the appropriate qualities and skills 'at the sharp end', all the energy and effort invested in the development of policy will fall short at the point of delivery. The international review team met a myriad of individuals with enormous commitment to their work, but their 'competence' appeared to derive more from that personal commitment than from any professional learning framework. Apart from obvious needs for those working with young people to understand requirements about issues such as health and safety or child protection, there is clearly also a need for a shared awareness of intervention strategies, curriculum development and methodological approaches. This calls for a training strategy which, in many areas of youth policy in Cyprus, appears not yet to have been developed.

6.3.4. Co-ordination

The issue of co-ordination is closely related to the integrated and cross-sectoral approach espoused by the Council of Europe (see above). A 'communication grid' that is both horizontal (across various levels of governance) and vertical (between different levels of governance) is essential if youth policy is to be directed appropriately, avoiding duplication or 'gaps'. At the level of national governance, the consultative intra-departmental committee fulfils an important co-ordination function, but lines of communication elsewhere, both vertically and horizontally, were less clear. The Cyprus Youth Board certainly occupies a key position in such processes, like a police officer directing traffic at a busy crossroads, representing the political will to those in the 'field' and absorbing their views through its advisory structures. This is, nevertheless, another issue that would repay more considered attention.

6.3.5. Cost

This is 'simply' a question of budget! Too often, policy aspirations and political rhetoric are not supported by sufficient resources. Indeed, the rhetoric often includes a statement that the question is not more money, but the more efficient use of existing resources. Clearly, as youth policy expands, more resources are required. Investing in young people, preferably through 'opportunity-focused' provision, but also through 'problem-orientated' intervention, is costly. The international review team welcomed the sustained and increased resourcing of the Cyprus Youth Board; such generous allocations (though no doubt they are 'never enough') certainly reflect the political commitment in Cyprus to youth policy.

6.4. The "D"s of youth policy development – a dynamic approach to youth policy formulation and execution

Through analysis of the ways in which 'youth policy' is developed and delivered, both in the countries that were the focus of early international reviews and beyond, a 'virtuous circle' model has been produced (see Figure 2).

At different points in this circle, the balance of the weight of the contribution by politicians, professionals and young people alters, though the input of all three remains essential. The cycle can start or stall at any point: it can start and be sustained through openness to new ideas and critical perspectives on existing ones; it will stall if there is not such receptivity.

Figure 2 A dynamic cycle for youth policy development

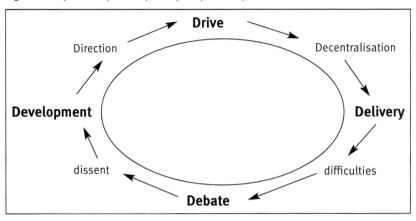

All youth policy needs a political champion, or 'driver'; without it, policy initiatives and the resourcing they require will grind to a halt. For policy to 'work on the ground' accurately at its target groups, it has to have structures and processes for effective delivery (the coverage, capacity and competence issues raised above). But the execution of any policy will encounter difficulties, which demand reflection and debate if practice is to be refined accordingly (this is part of the co-ordination issue above, if all relevant practioners are to contribute to the debate). There will almost certainly be differences of opinion within the ranks of professionals about how such challenges should be overcome. Sooner or later, however, debate has to stop and developmental work has to start, and this will be generally assumed to provide more calibrated and meaningful practice. This establishes some shift in direction, which then needs to enlist political support if new ideas and new measures are to be taken forward.

That is the outline of the model. It is an optimistic one, though it recognises that the circle can move slowly or indeed stop altogether. If appropriate structures are not in place, little can be delivered. If there is no facility for critical debate, practice will stagnate as times move on and needs change. If professionals (and young people) insist on debating forever, nothing will be developed. If there is little consensus about the direction policy should take, it is unlikely to secure political support.

There is currently strong political commitment in Cyprus to the idea of youth policy, and this commitment has been reflected internally by the work of the Cyprus Youth Board and externally by the invitation to the international review team to contribute to deliberations. There is, however, some concern expressed about delivery mechanisms, both the capacity and competence to fulfil the aspirations of government and young people. Forums for debate seem to remain restricted, just as the topics for debate appear to ignore some burning questions that demand attention (notably the situation of non-Greek Cypriot young people and a broad concept of multiculturalism). These limitations have the effect of paralysing, in part at least, the development of a youth policy consistent with the place of Cyprus within an enlarging Europe. Nevertheless, key planks for that development are in place, and the international review team hopes that the Cyprus Youth Board, through a more open debate and less politicised analysis, will continue to lead the youth policy field in that constructive direction.

7. Conclusion

The Cyprus Youth Board is certainly not standing still and has much to show for its work over the decade of its existence. As the international review team was exploring and deliberating on the Cyprus context, the Youth Board was engaged in a consultative process through the work of a number of thematic groups:

- Human rights
- Young professionals (students, trade unionists and young farmers)
- Active participation in decision-making
- Youth and culture
- Health
- Sports
- Disadvantage and disability
- The social involvement of young people
- Environment
- The National Youth Council

Many of these issues have been touched upon in this report; indeed, some early responses from these thematic groups have been included here. The international review team became increasingly aware that what is written for public consumption is not always what actually takes place, or even what different individuals and organisations want to take place. That should be no surprise, and part of youth policy development is to work within the creative space between them – closing down risk and negativity, and opening up opportunity and possibility.

Despite all the positive developments it encountered, the international review team felt there were still 'significant gaps' in knowledge and implementation, gaps that need to be addressed. Strengthening the relationship between research, policy and practice – in both directions – is an essential prerequisite for effective, coherent policy formulation and implementation.

Finally, as the international review team noted at the start of this report, the Cyprus Problem is never far from any debate in Cyprus. It consumes energy and constrains the possibility for full and frank discussion. Therefore it was of some reassurance to see that the Cyprus Youth Board, in its response to the EU White Paper question-naire on greater understanding of youth, courageously set out its views on the most important themes pertaining to young people in Cyprus:

- The integration of Turkish Cypriot youth in the Republic of Cyprus society
- The representation of ethnic communities in youth structures
- The role of young people in the resolution of the Cyprus issue
- Children: the near future of young people

(Cyprus Youth Board response to EU Youth White Paper questionnaire on greater understanding of youth, p. 11)

These are, indeed, at the heart of future youth policy developments in Cyprus. Before they are resolved, there are evidently immense psychological – as well as physical, political, historical, economic and cultural – barriers to be overcome. Nevertheless, the international review team met many people who were committed to moving in this direction. There was also a strong political commitment to establishing a more 'modern' youth policy framework in Cyprus, mediated through the extensively-praised work of the Cyprus Youth Board. It is to be hoped that this report has contributed to this process. The international review team does not pretend to have grasped all the detail and complexities of the Cyprus context. There will have been mistakes and misunderstandings, for which the team apologises, but it also asks those in Cyprus to consider the perspectives and challenges it has raised.

8. Recommendations

Recommendation 1

The international review team endorses the need for an 'unrestricted democratic dialogue' among young people, to determine their perspectives on the Cyprus Problem.

Recommendation 2

Given the de facto age range addressed under the banner of 'youth', consideration should be given to renaming the Cyprus Youth Board as the Cyprus Children and Youth Board – which reflects more accurately its frame of reference.

Recommendation 3

The vision for 'youth policy' in Cyprus needs to be more firmly delineated, identifying the guiding and governing themes within which the range of operational activity can be located.

Recommendation 4

The international review team believes that it would be timely for the Republic of Cyprus Government to consider amending the legal constitution of the Cyprus Youth Board in order to broaden the composition of its Governing/Administrative Board, to include representation beyond the established youth wings of the dominant political parties, and to set criteria for gender equality.

Recommendation 5

The international review team commends the initiative by the Cyprus Youth Board and the municipalities of Cyprus to establish municipal youth councils, but believes that these need to be based on greater autonomy and self-determination by youth NGOs and less constrained by the political framework which currently governs their existence.

Recommendation 6

The international review team applauds the development of a network of local youth clubs and centres, but believes these should be more firmly detached from local political influence and control, and that those who provide the programme of activities should have access to local-level training courses equipping them with the knowledge and skills of effective youth work.

Recommendation 7

The international review team commends the vision and ambition about such multifunctional centres. It acknowledges the considerable capital and revenue resources required for their development, but wholly supports the Cyprus Youth Board in its endeavour to secure the necessary funding.

Recommendation 8

The international review team believes strongly that information concerning the European YOUTH programme should be made available in both the official languages of Cyprus: Greek and Turkish. It also wishes to support the undertaking to have a mobile information base positioned in the Green Line at the checkpoint in Nicosia, which may encourage and assist young Turkish Cypriots in securing more equal access to participation in the different elements of the YOUTH programme.

Recommendation 9

The international review team remains unclear about the identity and status of the 'National Youth Council' of Cyprus. This demands further discussion and urgent clarification.

Recommendation 10

Though the international review team has not had sight of the Education Reform Committee's report, it feels that the arguments made both in the education chapter of the National Report and the practice model of the ZEP schools present a way forward for the much-needed reform of the (Greek) Cypriot education system. This is critical for intercultural learning and mutual understanding, though it is also likely to meet wider learning and development objectives.

Recommendation 11

The international review team felt that more attention needed to be given to the small, but steadily increasing, population of young people who are not Greek or Turkish Cypriots, in order to have more reliable data on their education and employment circumstances, and thereby to address any emergent issues.

Recommendation 12

The international review team welcomed the critical analysis of the current relationships between education and the labour market, produced by the University of Cyprus, and felt that its proposals were consistent with training and labour market initiatives which have been seen as a necessary component of 'youth policy' in other parts of Europe.

Recommendation 13

The international review team welcomes the infrastructure already in place for the development of non-formal learning opportunities for young people. It believes, however, that there needs to be a deeper exploration of the nature of provision and of the 'professional' skills applied by those who work with young people in this context.

Recommendation 14

The international review team encountered much progressive thinking about the health of young people in Cyprus and corresponding measures to address it. This work on policy and practice was, however, constrained by the absence of any overarching thinking about the weight (and therefore resources) to be attached to different issues, the most desired philosophies and methodologies, and connections between different health challenges, and also an imbalance in the data available. The production of a cross-departmental framework plan aimed at supporting the positive health of young people in Cyprus as well as combating health-risk behaviour would seem to be desirable. This might be entitled "The Health of the Young Nation".

Recommendation 15

In the Council of Europe guidelines on youth policy development (Council of Europe 2003b), there is a discussion of both a 'knowledge gap' and an 'implementation gap'. The former is the vacuum between research and policy, the second the vacuum between policy and practice. The international review team felt that there was a 'knowledge gap' in relation to (especially) non-Greek Cypriots and their housing, social protection and social welfare. This needs to be rectified before any 'implementation gap' can be considered.

Recommendation 16

The international review team believes that strengthened contact and engagement with diversity and difference across cultures, which is already starting through immigration and tourism as well as participation in the wider Europe, is an important catalyst for intercultural tolerance and understanding. It should, where possible, be supported and encouraged by the Cyprus Youth Board and other parts of the Republic of Cyprus Government.

Recommendation 17

The international review team was concerned to read, in the draft National Report, the somewhat damning critique of the current youth justice system in Cyprus. It welcomes the initiatives being taken through the Parliamentary Committee on Criminal Affairs in relation to more constructive approaches to dealing with young offenders and believes that such a trajectory should be pursued.

Recommendation 18

The international review team is aware that inter-religious dialogue in many parts of the world can represent a powerful platform for peace education and intercultural learning. In Cyprus it could also be a basis for the promotion of tolerance and understanding.

Recommendation 19

The international review team believes that the principles of youth participation in Cyprus are well articulated and that the basis for good practice has been established. This now needs to be consolidated and developed – and particular attention given to some legitimate criticisms concerning the place and voice of less organised and less politicised young people.

Recommendation 20

The international review team notes the increasing interest and commitment in Cyprus to the 'active engagement' and 'social involvement' of young people. It also notes, however, the absence of a coherent framework for such development. It rec-

> Recommendations

ommends, therefore, that consideration should be given to a more robust strategy for volunteering, in the interests of both 'hosting' organisations and presenting volunteers, drawing on model already in existence elsewhere in Europe.

Recommendation 21

The international review team feels that the Cyprus Youth Board and others need to give greater attention to the specific needs of 'minority' groups of young people, such as those with disabilities or those with alternative sexual orientation.

Recommendation 22

The international review team recommends a more thorough scrutiny to ensure that access to a range of constructive social opportunities is not obstructed, for particular social groups of young people, by barriers which may not be readily apparent to the 'dominant mind'. Only through so doing will the risks of increasing levels of social exclusion, especially among more marginal and disadvantaged groups, be minimised.

Recommendation 23

The international review team would suggest, as youth information services proliferate in Cyprus, that a formal national 'ethics committee' be constituted in order to ensure that the information made available through leaflets or through any on-line service is validated for its accuracy, balance and fairness.

Recommendation 24

The international review team recommends an early exploration of the types of young people making use of youth information provision, and the reasons they are doing so. Despite their evident strengths and qualities, this would provide an 'early warning' system for addressing any emergent challenges or problems.

Recommendation 25

The Council of Europe has a long track record in the development of materials for intercultural learning and human rights education. These should be used for supporting the emergent desire in Cyprus to respond positively to the relatively new challenges it faces in terms of its increasingly multicultural population.

Recommendation 26

The international review team felt that the European Commission, in consultation with the national agency for Cyprus, and the Cyprus Youth Board, should explore how best to overcome barriers to participation in EU youth programmes for Turkish Cypriots and thereby provide as equal an opportunity as possible for all Cypriots, irrespective of their place of residence.

Recommendation 27

The international review team believes that, as young Cypriots take an increasing part in a variety of European youth programmes, a 'network infrastructure' needs to be established, so that they can both consolidate and disseminate the learning they have gained.

Recommendation 28

The international review team believes that the relationships between research, policy and practice need to be strengthened in order to contest and clarify the 'evidence' on which youth policy is constructed.

Recommendation 29

The international review team believes that a modest (at first) training framework for those who work with young people across a range of youth policy domains needs to be considered. This would not be concerned with 'high level' professional qualifications (such as counselling or psychology), but with the core components of developing and delivering effective practice, through building relationships and cultivating the motivation of young people.

Recommendation 30

The international review team believes that an opportunity needs to be created, both within and across substantive areas of youth policy, for policy-makers, researchers and practitioners to share both theoretical and empirical ideas about effective practice. To this end, a 'communication strategy' needs to be formulated.

Bibliography

Council of Europe (2003a), Experts on Youth Policy Indicators: third and concluding meeting, Strasbourg: European Youth Centre.

Council of Europe (2003b), Select Committee of Experts on the Establishment of Guidelines for the Formulation and Implementation of Youth Policies: final report, Strasbourg: Council of Europe.

Edwards, G., Anderson, P., Babor, T., Caswell, S., Ferrence, R., Giesbrecht, N., Godfrey, C., Holder, H., Lemmens, P., Makela, K., Midanik, L., Nostrom, T., Osterberg, E., Romero, A., Room, R., Simpura, J. and Skog, O. (1994), Alcohol Policy and the Public Good, New York: Oxford University Press.

European Commission (2001), A New Impetus for European Youth: White Paper, Brussels: European Commission.

Evans, J. (2003), Youth Policy in Malta, Strasbourg: Council of Europe.

Jones, G. and Wallace, C. (1992), Youth, Family and Citizenship, Milton Keynes, UK: Open University Press.

Lauritzen, P. and Guidikova, I. (2002), "European youth development and policy: the role of NGOs and public authority in the making of the European citizen", Handbook of Applied Developmental Science, Vol. 3, pp. 363-382.

Rutter, M. and Smith, D. (eds) (1995), Psychosocial Disorders in Young People: time trends and their causes, Chichester, UK: Wiley.

Williamson, H. (1999), Youth Policy in Finland, Strasbourg: Council of Europe.

Williamson, H. (2002), Supporting Young People in Europe: principles, policy and practice, Strasbourg: Council of Europe.

Documents consulted

Apanemi – Women's Information and Support Centre (various documentation).

Bi-Communal Youth Forum, Common Declarations.

Council of Europe, Parliamentary Assembly, "The demographic structure of Cyprus, 1992".

Council of Europe, Report by Mr Alvaro Gil-Robles, the Commissioner for Human Rights, on his visit to Cyprus 25-29 June 2003.

Cyprus Anti-Drugs Council, leaflets.

Cyprus Family Planning Association, Presentations on culture, volunteerism.

Cyprus Government, "Current programmes on youth-related issues".

Cyprus Government, "Government policy vis-à-vis the Turkish Cypriots", 30 April 2003.

Cyprus Youth Board documents:

- Law
- Leaflet
- Structure
- Board and staff
- Budget, 2004
- Drugs helpline
- Strategic plan, 1999-2003
- Members of the intra-departmental consultative committee
- Governance Programme of the President on youth policy
- Membership of the Advisory Body
- List of research conducted by the Youth Board

Cyprus Youth Board, responses to the Open Method of Co-ordination on the European Union White Paper on Youth Policy:

- Participation
- Information

- Voluntary activities
- Greater understanding of youth

Cyprus Youth Board, thematic consultations on youth policy formulation, see Documents arising.

- Culture (Cyprus FPA)
- Culture (TKP Youth Branch)
- Equality (Intercultural Centre)
- Health: sexual and reproductive health, teen pregnancy, HIV/AIDS
- National Youth Councils
- Participation (working group)
- Social involvement (Intercultural Centre)
- Social involvement (working group), including "Proposal on youth social involvement"
- Voluntary activities (PPP presentation by Cyprus FPA)

Cyprus Youth Board, "Youth of Cyprus – free time, work, relationships, perceptions and problems", 2002.

Demetriades, E., "Survey on active participation of youth in Cypriot society", 2001 (plus Appendix: Questionnaire on participation).

Democratic Rally (DISY), documents.

draft National report, see University of Cyprus

Democratic Rally (DISY)

Documents arising from the Cyprus Youth Board thematic consultations on youth policy formulation:

- Cyprus Youth Policy formulation – Culture (Cyprus FPA)
- Cyprus Youth Policy formulation – Culture (TKP Youth Branch)
- Cyprus Youth Policy formulation – Equality (Intercultural Centre)
- Cyprus Youth Policy formulation – Health: sexual and reproductive health, teen pregnancy, HIV/AIDS
- Cyprus Youth Policy formulation – Participation (working group)
- Cyprus Youth Policy formulation – Social involvement (Intercultural Centre)
- Cyprus Youth Policy formulation – Social involvement (working group)
- Cyprus Youth Policy formulation – Voluntary activities (PPP presentation by Cyprus FPA)
- National Youth Councils

DZF, Memorandum on the Republic of Cyprus boycott of sustainability forum, 25 October 2004.

EDEK (Social Democrats), documents.

Intercultural Centre of Cyprus, "Proposal for the development of a national youth policy of Cyprus" (themes: social involvement; equality, human rights, social inclusion and intercultural dialogue).

International review team, Notes from first visit.

International review team, Notes from second visit.

Ministry of Health, HIV/AIDS strategic plan, 2004-8.

National Agency for Cyprus, Priorities for the YOUTH programme.

National Report, see University of Cyprus.

Notes from first visit by international review team.

Notes from second visit by international review team.

Opening welcome speech to the international review team by the chairman of the House Standing Conference on Criminal Affairs 1st June 2004.

Open Therapeutic Community, General Population Survey, 2003.

Our Concept of Socialism

Parliament of Cyprus, Opening welcome speech to the international review team by the chairman of the House Standing Conference on Criminal Affairs, 1 June 2004.

Press and Information Office of the Republic of Cyprus Government, website:

- Mass media
- Turkish press
- Cultural heritage
- The 10-point agreement
- The rights of Turkish Cypriot employees
- No embargo against the Turkish Cypriots
- Turkey did not have the right of intervention
- Latest developments on the Cyprus Problem
- A brief history of the PIO
- EU-Cyprus Joint Parliamentary Committee

Press and Information Office of the Republic of Cyprus Government, "About Cyprus", 2001.

Press and Information Office of the Republic of Cyprus Government, "European stand on the Cyprus problem".

Press and Information Office of the Republic of Cyprus Government, "The Cyprus Question".

press cuttings, various British press cuttings on the referendum on the Annan Plan.

Republic of Cyprus, see Cyprus Government; Ministry of Health; Press and Information Office.

Republic of Cyprus Government, Government Policy vis a vis the Turkish Cypriots 30th April 2003

Survey on Active Participation of the Youth in Cypriot Society [plus Appendix: Questionnaire on Participation]

[Socialist Party of Cyprus], "Our concept of socialism".

Taki, Y., "Are witch hunts part of the European solution", *Sunday Mail*, 24 October 2004.

TKP Youth Branch, Presentation on culture.

University of Cyprus, draft National Report on Youth Policy in Cyprus:

- History
- Education
- Employment and Training
- Health
- Crime
- Culture
- Conclusions and Recommendations

Various (British) press cuttings on the referendum on the Annan Plan

Youth Board of Cyprus responses to the Open Method of Co-ordination on the European Union White Paper on youth policy:

Youth Board, see Cyprus Youth Board

- Participation
- Information
- Voluntary activities
- Greater understanding of youth

Sales agents for publications of the Council of Europe
Agents de vente des publications du Conseil de l'Europe

BELGIUM/BELGIQUE
La Librairie Européenne -
The European Bookshop
Rue de l'Orme, 1
B-1040 BRUXELLES
Tel.: +32 (0)2 231 04 35
Fax: +32 (0)2 735 08 60
E-mail: order@libeurop.be
http://www.libeurop.be

Jean De Lannoy
Avenue du Roi 202 Koningslaan
B-1190 BRUXELLES
Tel.: +32 (0)2 538 43 08
Fax: +32 (0)2 538 08 41
E-mail: jean.de.lannoy@dl-servi.com
http://www.jean-de-lannoy.be

CANADA
Renouf Publishing Co. Ltd.
1-5369 Canotek Road
OTTAWA, Ontario K1J 9J3, Canada
Tel.: +1 613 745 2665
Fax: +1 613 745 7660
Toll-Free Tel.: (866) 767-6766
E-mail: order.dept@renoufbooks.com
http://www.renoufbooks.com

**CZECH REPUBLIC/
RÉPUBLIQUE TCHÈQUE**
Suweco CZ, s.r.o.
Klecakova 347
CZ-180 21 PRAHA 9
Tel.: +420 2 424 59 204
Fax: +420 2 848 21 646
E-mail: import@suweco.cz
http://www.suweco.cz

DENMARK/DANEMARK
GAD
Vimmelskaftet 32
DK-1161 KØBENHAVN K
Tel.: +45 77 66 60 00
Fax: +45 77 66 60 01
E-mail: gad@gad.dk
http://www.gad.dk

FINLAND/FINLANDE
Akateeminen Kirjakauppa
PO Box 128
Keskuskatu 1
FIN-00100 HELSINKI
Tel.: +358 (0)9 121 4430
Fax: +358 (0)9 121 4242
E-mail: akatilaus@akateeminen.com
http://www.akateeminen.com

FRANCE
La Documentation française
(diffusion/distribution France entière)
124, rue Henri Barbusse
F-93308 AUBERVILLIERS CEDEX
Tél.: +33 (0)1 40 15 70 00
Fax: +33 (0)1 40 15 68 00
E-mail: commande@ladocumentationfrancaise.fr
http://www.ladocumentationfrancaise.fr

Librairie Kléber
1 rue des Francs Bourgeois
F-67000 STRASBOURG
Tel.: +33 (0)3 88 15 78 88
Fax: +33 (0)3 88 15 78 80
E-mail: francois.wolfermann@librairie-kleber.fr
http://www.librairie-kleber.com

**GERMANY/ALLEMAGNE
AUSTRIA/AUTRICHE**
UNO Verlag GmbH
August-Bebel-Allee 6
D-53175 BONN
Tel.: +49 (0)228 94 90 20
Fax: +49 (0)228 94 90 222
E-mail: bestellung@uno-verlag.de
http://www.uno-verlag.de

GREECE/GRÈCE
Librairie Kauffmann s.a.
Stadiou 28
GR-105 64 ATHINAI
Tel.: +30 210 32 55 321
Fax.: +30 210 32 30 320
E-mail: ord@otenet.gr
http://www.kauffmann.gr

HUNGARY/HONGRIE
Euro Info Service kft.
1137 Bp. Szent István krt. 12.
H-1137 BUDAPEST
Tel.: +36 (06)1 329 2170
Fax: +36 (06)1 349 2053
E-mail: euroinfo@euroinfo.hu
http://www.euroinfo.hu

ITALY/ITALIE
Licosa SpA
Via Duca di Calabria, 1/1
I-50125 FIRENZE
Tel.: +39 0556 483215
Fax: +39 0556 41257
E-mail: licosa@licosa.com
http://www.licosa.com

MEXICO/MEXIQUE
Mundi-Prensa México, S.A. De C.V.
Río Pánuco, 141 Delegacion Cuauhtémoc
06500 MÉXICO, D.F.
Tel.: +52 (01)55 55 33 56 58
Fax: +52 (01)55 55 14 67 99
E-mail: mundiprensa@mundiprensa.com.mx
http://www.mundiprensa.com.mx

NETHERLANDS/PAYS-BAS
De Lindeboom Internationale Publicaties b.v.
M.A. de Ruyterstraat 20 A
NL-7482 BZ HAAKSBERGEN
Tel.: +31 (0)53 5740004
Fax: +31 (0)53 5729296
E-mail: books@delindeboom.com
http://www.delindeboom.com

NORWAY/NORVÈGE
Akademika
Postboks 84 Blindern
N-0314 OSLO
Tel.: +47 2 218 8100
Fax: +47 2 218 8103
E-mail: support@akademika.no
http://www.akademika.no

POLAND/POLOGNE
Ars Polona JSC
25 ul. Obroncόw
PL-03-933 WARSZAWA
Tel.: +48 (0)22 509 86 00
Fax: +48 (0)22 509 86 10
E-mail: arspolona@arspolona.com.pl
http://www.arspolona.com.pl

PORTUGAL
Livraria Portugal
(Dias & Andrade, Lda.)
Rua do Carmo, 70
P-1200-094 LISBOA
Tel.: +351 21 347 42 82 / 85
Fax: +351 21 347 02 64
E-mail: info@livrariaportugal.pt
http://www.livrariaportugal.pt

**RUSSIAN FEDERATION/
FÉDÉRATION DE RUSSIE**
Ves Mir
9a, Kolpacnhyi per.
RU-101000 MOSCOW
Tel.: +7 (8)495 623 6839
Fax: +7 (8)495 625 4269
E-mail: orders@vesmirbooks.ru
http://www.vesmirbooks.ru

SPAIN/ESPAGNE
Mundi-Prensa Libros, s.a.
Castelló, 37
E-28001 MADRID
Tel.: +34 914 36 37 00
Fax: +34 915 75 39 98
E-mail: libreria@mundiprensa.es
http://www.mundiprensa.com

SWITZERLAND/SUISSE
Van Diermen Editions – ADECO
Chemin du Lacuez 41
CH-1807 BLONAY
Tel.: +41 (0)21 943 26 73
Fax: +41 (0)21 943 36 05
E-mail: info@adeco.org
http://www.adeco.org

UNITED KINGDOM/ROYAUME-UNI
The Stationery Office Ltd
PO Box 29
GB-NORWICH NR3 1GN
Tel.: +44 (0)870 600 5522
Fax: +44 (0)870 600 5533
E-mail: book.enquiries@tso.co.uk
http://www.tsoshop.co.uk

**UNITED STATES and CANADA/
ÉTATS-UNIS et CANADA**
Manhattan Publishing Company
468 Albany Post Road
CROTTON-ON-HUDSON, NY 10520, USA
Tel.: +1 914 271 5194
Fax: +1 914 271 5856
E-mail: Info@manhattanpublishing.com
http://www.manhattanpublishing.com

Council of Europe Publishing/Editions du Conseil de l'Europe
F-67075 Strasbourg Cedex
Tel.: +33 (0)3 88 41 25 81 – Fax: +33 (0)3 88 41 39 10 – E-mail: publishing@coe.int – Website: http://book.coe.int